FRIENDLY FAMILY HAPPY HOME

Home Is The Heart Of Dream, Dignity, Direction, And Destiny

BY
SYAVIHA MULENGYA

This book is a gift

From:_____

To:_____

On:_____

Personal Comments

_____

_____

_____

_____

_____

Thank you God for your goodness, grace
and the gift you have bestowed upon me

DEDICATION

- To my late parents, Samuel Mahamba and Elizabeth Vahingania, thank you for loving, listening and leading me in the ways of God.

- My brothers and sisters, Moi9se, Samson, Schandrack, Semu, Seriba, Yerusi, Desize, Kahambu and Katungu Mulengya, thank you for teaching me the values of hope, humility and hard work.

- To my mentors, Janine and Sid Phillips, thank you for your inspiration, instruction and information. You always encourage and believe in my vision.

- To Devin and Christine Walker, you have motivated me to serve, seek and stay close to God. Thank you for your wisdom and the great work you are doing.

- To my queen Rafiki Kavuya Syaviha, thank you for standing, supporting and serving with me in hard and good times. You are my miracle.

- To my lovely daughters, Blessed and Best and Brilliance, you always encourage, excite and enjoy my work. You are my greatest inspiration.

- To my friends and fans, you always advise, appreciate and assist me in this noble work. Thank you for the financial support.

Table of Contents

INTRODUCTION

The home is a foundational place where our dreams, destiny, direction, and dignity are shaped. Dreams are nurtured within a loving and caring home where family members inspire one another to believe in their potential. A supportive home encourages children and adults to dream big and work toward their goals with confidence. **Psalm 127:1** teaches us, *"Unless the Lord builds the house, the builders labor in vain."* This verse reminds us that a home grounded in God's love creates a strong foundation for hope to grow and flourish. When family members encourage each other to pursue their dreams, they build an environment where everyone feels supported and motivated to take steps toward their future.

A strong home also provides the tools to turn dreams into reality. Parents and family members can guide each other by sharing wisdom and offering encouragement along the way. **Proverbs 16:3** says, *"Commit to the Lord whatever you do, and He will establish your plans."* Simple acts of kindness, such as cheering someone on or reminding them of their strengths, inspire confidence and determination. By nurturing dreams together, the family builds a foundation of trust and teamwork, making the home a special place where aspirations grow into achievements.

The home also plays an important role in shaping our destiny. It is within the family that we learn important values, morals, and life lessons. Parents and guardians guide their children by teaching them to make wise choices and helping them discover their God-given purpose. **Proverbs 22:6** reminds us, *"Start children off on the way they should go, and even when they are old they will not turn from it."* By providing structure and spiritual guidance, the home prepares every family member to walk confidently on the path that leads to their destiny.

Moreover, the home sets the direction for life. It is where we learn how to face challenges, solve problems, and stay focused on what matters most. When a home emphasizes love, unity, and respect, it creates a sense of purpose and clarity for everyone. **Proverbs 3:5-6** says, *"Trust in the Lord with all your heart and lean not on your own understanding; in all your ways submit to Him, and He will make your paths straight."* A home rooted in faith provides direction, helping family members navigate life's ups and downs with strength and trust in God.

Finally, the home is a place where dignity is built and protected. It is where we learn to respect ourselves and others. The values taught at home shape how we treat others and how we see ourselves. **Proverbs 24:3** says, *"By wisdom a house is built, and through understanding it is established."* A loving home creates an environment where dignity thrives—where every member feels valued and respected. This sense of self-worth helps us carry ourselves with confidence in the world. Ultimately, the home is a sanctuary where dreams are born, destinies are shaped, direction is provided, and dignity is preserved, making it the heart of our lives.

Home is The Foundation

The purpose of home is profound and transformative, making it one of life's greatest blessings. Home matters so much because it is not just a place to live; it is the heart of dreams, destiny, direction, and dignity. It is where love, faith, and shared values take root, creating an environment that nurtures the body, mind, and soul. **Psalm 127:1** reminds us, *"Unless the Lord builds the house, the builders labor in vain."* This verse shows us that a home centered on God is the cornerstone of a meaningful and fulfilling life.

A loving home is the starting point of life's journey. It is where we first learn about love, kindness, honesty, and humility, shaping the values that guide us. **Proverbs 22:6** says, *"Train up a child in the way he should go, and when he is old, he will not depart from it."* Home is a sacred space where parents and family teach the principles that honor God's truth and provide strength in times of uncertainty. These lessons prepare us to step into the world with confidence, knowing that we are deeply loved and supported.

Home also offers refuge, safety, and peace, creating a haven for our hearts and souls. It is where God's presence calms our fears and gives us the security we need to grow. **Proverbs 18:10** reminds us, *"The name of the Lord is a fortified tower; the righteous run to it and are safe."* A safe home reflects God's protection, allowing every family member to feel shielded from life's challenges and renewed in His love. When love, faith, and unity are at the center, home becomes a place of serenity—a reflection of God's kingdom.

Ultimately, the purpose of home is to glorify God by nurturing relationships, strengthening family bonds, and sharing values. It is the foundation where dreams are dreamed, destinies are shaped, and lives are transformed. A home filled with God's love and truth empowers us to live with purpose and inspires others to do the same. With God as the builder, home is not just a shelter—it is the heart of joy, meaning, and hope for all who dwell within.

1

WHY HOME MATTERS SO MUCH

1. Starting Point

H ome is where life begins. It is the place where our journey starts, laying the foundation for everything we will become. It is within these walls that we first experience the love and care of those who surround us. **Psalm 127:1** reminds us, *"Unless the Lord builds the house, the builders labor in vain."* This verse tells us that a home's true strength and purpose come from God's presence within it. Home is not just made of bricks and mortar—it is a sacred starting point where identity, faith, and values are formed.

At home, we learn our first lessons about love, trust, and relationships. These lessons shape how we view ourselves and how we interact with others. Home is where the seeds of kindness, patience, and forgiveness are planted, helping us to grow into the people God designed us to be. Through the guidance and care of family, home becomes a training ground where we are prepared to face life's challenges with strength and confidence.

SYAVIHA MULENGYA

The purpose of a home goes beyond its physical aspects; it is a safe place where we can develop spiritually and emotionally. Here, we learn about God's love and His faithfulness. Our parents or caregivers often teach us to pray, to trust, and to rely on His wisdom. These spiritual foundations provide the stability we need as we step out into the world, knowing that God walks with us wherever we go.

Home also teaches us the importance of connection and togetherness. Through shared meals, conversations, and laughter, we experience the joy of being part of a family. It is a place of belonging where we feel valued and supported. No matter where life takes us, the lessons and memories from home remain with us, guiding us and giving us comfort.

Above all, home matters because it gives us a starting point filled with love, safety, and purpose. It is where we are nurtured, molded, and prepared to pursue the calling that God has placed on our lives. When God is at the center of our home, it becomes a place of incredible blessing, equipping us to build a future filled with faith, hope, and joy.

2. Sense of Belonging

Home is the place where we truly experience a deep sense of belonging. It is where we are loved unconditionally and accepted just as we are. **Romans 12:10** says, *"Be devoted to one another in love. Honor one another above yourselves."* This verse reminds us of the selfless love that strengthens the bonds within our family, ensuring that no one ever feels alone. At home, this devotion creates an environment where every individual feels valued, cared for, and supported. It's a sacred space that welcomes us warmly and encourages us to thrive.

The belonging we find at home nurtures both our hearts and minds. It provides comfort during times of uncertainty and assurance during moments of doubt. A loving home creates a strong foundation for growth, offering us a community where we can express ourselves freely without fear. Even in challenging circumstances, home becomes a haven—a refuge where we are reminded of our worth and understood with compassion. This sense of belonging is like a gentle embrace, reminding us that we are deeply cherished.

When a home is built on love, it reflects the beauty of God's kingdom—a place where His children are united by grace and peace. This connection restores hope and reminds us of the unique purpose God has for each of us in His greater plan. A loving home allows us to experience His presence in the love we share with our family, reaffirming that we are part of something eternal and meaningful. By nurturing this sense of belonging, we honor God and build a legacy of love that strengthens generations to come.

3. Strengthening Bonds

Home is the sacred place where relationships grow stronger. It is the heart of love, care, and connection within a family. **Ecclesiastes 4:12** says, *"A cord of three strands is not quickly broken."* This verse beautifully shows the strength of unity and how bonds become unbreakable when they are rooted in love and faith. Home is where shared moments, whether joyful or difficult, create a foundation of resilience. Through laughter, tears, and lessons learned, families grow closer and stand together.

In a loving home, forgiveness flows naturally, and grace is abundant. No family is perfect, and disagreements or mistakes happen, but a home built on love allows relationships to heal and thrive. Communication, patience, and trust are the pillars that hold these connections strong. This atmosphere of love and forgiveness reflects God's grace toward us, reminding everyone in the family of His endless and unconditional love.

The strength of bonds at home extends beyond day-to-day interactions. These relationships prepare us to face life's challenges together, with unwavering support from those who care for us most. Strong family ties serve as a reminder that we are never alone, no matter what we go through. This unity also mirrors God's perfect design for family, where every member has a role in uplifting one another.

Most importantly, strengthening family bonds fulfills God's purpose for love and unity. He designed families to stand firm together, offering support and encouragement through every season of life. When we nurture these relationships at home, we are living out His divine plan and creating a space where everyone feels valued, supported, and truly loved.

4. Self-Discovery

Home is where we begin the journey of self-discovery, a space where we uncover who we are and embrace the gifts God has given us. **Psalm 139:14** reminds us, *"I praise you because I am fearfully and wonderfully made; your works are wonderful, I know that full well."* These words highlight that each of us is uniquely created by God, and home is the haven where we can explore His wonderful design for our lives. At home, we are encouraged to recognize our strengths, talents, and personalities, growing into the individuals God has called us to be.

Through the love and encouragement of family, we gain confidence in our identity and purpose. Home provides the nurturing environment where we can test our abilities, learn new skills, and discover what makes us special. The lessons learned at home—from kindness to perseverance—shape our character and set us on a path toward fulfilling God's plan. It's in this environment that we develop a sense of belonging and begin to understand our value as part of His creation.

The benefits of self-discovery at home go beyond recognizing our talents. Home teaches us to see ourselves through God's eyes, building humility and self-awareness. It helps us understand that we are His masterpiece, designed for a unique purpose in His kingdom. These moments of reflection and growth remind us that God has a plan for each of us, and our journey begins with the love and guidance of our family.

Home also matters because it instills values that guide us throughout life. It is within this space that we learn to love, respect, and serve others, reflecting God's teachings in our relationships. The foundation laid at home equips us to navigate challenges and make decisions with integrity. As we grow, we carry these lessons with us, impacting not only our own lives but also those of others.

Ultimately, home is a place of transformation, where God's blessings are evident in the growth and unity of the family. It becomes a sacred space that nurtures love, builds confidence, and encourages us to shine in the world. The lessons and experiences from home give us the courage to step into the future, knowing that we are fearfully and wonderfully made by God to fulfill His purpose. Home matters most because it is where the journey of knowing ourselves and living for God begins.

5. Sympathy

Home is the birthplace of sympathy, where we learn to care for others. **Galatians 6:2** teaches, *"Carry each other's burdens, and in this way, you will fulfill the law of Christ."* At home, we experience compassion and kindness that ripple outward into the world.

In a loving family, we are taught the value of empathy by witnessing it firsthand. We learn to listen, support, and understand others with open hearts. This foundation of sympathy prepares us to extend God's love to those in need.

Sympathy matters because it makes us vessels of grace. When home nurtures compassion, we are equipped to spread hope, healing, and love to everyone we encounter.

6. Significance and Meaning

Home is where we begin to understand the significance of our lives. It is not just a physical place; It helps us see the role we play in God's plan and gives our existence meaning. Jeremiah 29:11 reassures us, "For I know the plans I have for you," declares the Lord, "plans to prosper you and not to harm you, plans to give you hope and a future." This verse reminds us that God has designed each of us for a specific purpose, and home is where this understanding starts to unfold. Within its walls, we are prepared for the journey of life and reminded that we are created with hope and a future.

Home is a place where values are taught and modeled. Whether it's kindness, honesty, patience, or forgiveness, the lessons we learn at home guide us throughout our lives. In a meaningful home, these values are not just words—they are lived out in actions. A mother's compassion, a father's wisdom, or a sibling's encouragement all demonstrate the importance of love and respect. Every shared moment—from mealtimes to heartfelt conversations—creates lasting memories that remind us of our worth and purpose. These memories become part of who we are, shaping our character and inspiring us to live according to God's truth.

At home, we also discover the importance of family and faith. Family is the foundation of love and support, helping us feel connected and valued. It's within this safe space that we can grow in faith, learning to trust God's guidance and to seek His will for our lives. Home becomes a spiritual sanctuary where prayer, worship, and reflection deepen our relationship with God. As we experience unconditional love from our family, we are reminded of God's eternal love for us—a love that is unchanging and all-encompassing. Through family and faith, home becomes a place where we find strength, hope, and inspiration.

When home is filled with significance and meaning, it becomes a reflection of God's eternal promise. It reminds us that He is faithful and that His plan for us is good. The love and peace we experience at home are glimpses of God's kingdom—a place where we are cherished and cared for. This sense of belonging gives us confidence to face life's challenges, knowing that we are part of something greater than ourselves. Home anchors us in hope, renewing our trust in God's purpose for our lives.

Ultimately, home matters because it shapes our understanding of who we are and why we exist. It is where we learn to embrace God's calling and live with purpose. A home filled with love, faith, and meaning becomes a sacred place where hearts are nurtured, lives are transformed, and God's promises are fulfilled. With God at the center, home becomes not just a place to live, but a foundation for a life rooted in hope and significance.

7. Safety

Home is a special place where we find safety and refuge, offering protection for our hearts and minds. It reflects the promise in **Proverbs 18:10:** *"The name of the Lord is a fortified tower; the righteous run to it and are safe."* Just as God provides shelter through His love, a loving home mirrors this by creating a space where we feel cared for and supported. It allows us to rest and feel secure, giving us the strength to face life's challenges.

Safety at home goes beyond physical protection; it includes emotional and spiritual security as well. At home, we can express ourselves freely without fear of judgment, knowing we are surrounded by understanding and love. It becomes a refuge where we can heal, grow, and connect with God. With family and faith at the center, home transforms into a sanctuary, helping us feel comforted and grounded during hard times.

Ultimately, a safe home gives us peace of mind and reminds us that God is our ultimate protector. Even when life feels uncertain, the security we experience at home is a reflection of His constant care and watchfulness over us. This makes home a true haven—a place where love, faith, and peace are always present, giving us the courage and hope to move forward.

8. Shared Values

Home is the foundation where shared values are taught and lived out. It is within the home that principles such as love, kindness, honesty, and humility are first introduced and practiced. These values guide how we treat others and how we navigate the world. **Proverbs 22:6** *reminds us, "Train up a child in the way he should go, and when he is old, he will not depart from it." This verse highlights* *the importance of instilling strong moral foundations in children at home, ensuring that these lessons stay with them throughout life.*

Shared values at home create a sense of unity and serve as a compass for making decisions. When a family aligns itself with God's truth, it develops a clear sense of right and wrong, making it easier to navigate life's challenges together. By living out these values, families shine as lights in the world, reflecting God's love and grace. Through kindness, forgiveness, and faith, a family demonstrates to others what it means to live with purpose and integrity.

A home filled with shared values has the power to inspire and empower every member of the family. It reminds each person of their God-given purpose and equips them to face the world with confidence. When love, faith, and humility are the foundation, the home becomes a place where individuals grow into who God created them to be. In this way, the values nurtured at home do not just remain within the family—they ripple outward to bless and glorify God in the wider community.

9. Serenity

Home is where true serenity and peace can be found. It is a place that reflects God's promise in **Isaiah 26:3:** *"You will keep in perfect peace those whose minds are steadfast, because they trust in you."* When we trust in God and keep Him at the center of our home, it becomes a space where His presence is deeply felt. A peaceful home calms our worries and fears, offering a refuge from the challenges of life. This peace allows us to focus on love and gratitude, bringing our hearts closer to God.

Serenity in the home comes through the bonds of family, shared love, and moments of prayer. Whether it's sitting quietly together, worshiping God, or simply supporting each other, these acts create a calm environment that restores our souls. A serene home reflects God's kingdom, where love, faith, and harmony reign. It is a place of renewal, reminding us that with God's presence, peace is always within reach. Through His grace, home becomes a sanctuary where we can find comfort, hope, and strength to move forward.

10. Shelter and Security

Home is the shelter and security we all need. It is the place where we feel safe, loved, and protected. **Psalm 91:1** says, *"Whoever dwells in the shelter of the Most High will rest in the shadow of the Almighty."* This verse reminds us that just as God provides us with His protection, our home offers a similar refuge. It is where we find comfort and strength to face life's struggles. Home becomes a space where we can rest and recharge, knowing we are cared for and supported.

The security of a home is more than just physical safety. It also gives us emotional and spiritual protection. At home, we feel free to express ourselves without fear of being judged. It is a place where understanding, love, and kindness are present. A safe home allows us to heal when we are hurt and to grow into the people God has called us to be. The peace we experience within a secured home strengthens our confidence and helps us face challenges with courage.

A home filled with God's love provides the ultimate protection. His presence brings peace to every corner, reminding us that we are never alone. When our home is built on faith and love, it becomes a special place where we can experience God's care in a proper way. This spiritual safety reassures us during tough times and fills our hearts with trust in His promises.

In the shelter of home, we see the blessings of God's provision. It is a place of warmth, love, and unity. The care and protection we receive at home remind us of God's promise to always watch over us. Home is where we can take refuge, renew our spirits, and be reminded of His never-ending grace. It is truly a gift and a blessing, meant to be cherished and valued deeply.

2

TREASURE YOUR FAMILY

Home is one of life's greatest treasures, a gift from God that should be cherished and valued deeply. It is where love and memories are built, and its worth goes far beyond material possessions. **Matthew 6:21** says, *"For where your treasure is, there your heart will be also."* Treasuring your home means placing your heart into it—thinking highly of its significance, treating family members with kindness, and always seeking to make it a place filled with joy and peace. By valuing your home and everyone in it, you create an environment where love and faith thrive, reflecting God's blessings.

Our home is a precious place, and you have an important role to play in making it an amazing place. God placed you in your family for a reason, and your presence matters more than you may realize. As part of your home, you are either building it up or breaking it down with your actions and words. **Proverbs 14:1** says, *"The wise woman builds her house, but with her own hands the foolish one tears hers down."* This shows us that our attitude and efforts make a big difference. Your home's peace is also your peace, so take responsibility to make it a place of love, understanding, and harmony. Value, love, treasure, and protect your home because it is the foundation for your life and relationships.

You are part of the solution to the challenges your home may face. Mistakes happen, and no family is perfect, but your efforts can help bring healing and unity. Praise God for placing you in your family, even if you sometimes wonder why. **Jeremiah 29:11** reminds us, *"For I know the plans I have for you," declares the Lord, "plans to prosper you and not to harm you, plans to give you hope and a future."* God doesn't make mistakes; He knows why He placed you in your family, and He wants to see you shine and set a good example. Take charge of your role in the family, knowing that your attitude and actions can bring about positive change and inspire others.

You are an ambassador of your home, representing your family wherever you go. **Your behavior reflects the values you learned at home, and people will notice where you come from based on how you carry yourself.** When you live with integrity, kindness, and respect, you honor your family and show the world the love of God. Even if your home is not perfect, don't be ashamed of it. Pray and ask God for wisdom on how to bring positive change. Your love and dedication to your home can make it a place of joy, peace, and purpose.

*Start by changing your attitude toward your home. Instead of focusing on its flaws, thank God for it and trust Him to guide you in making it bette*r. **1 Thessalonians 5:18** says, *"Give thanks in all circumstances; for this is God ' s will for you in Christ Jesus."* Love your family and appreciate the unique bond you share. Spend time with them, talk to them kindly, and build stronger relationships.

Your home is a treasure, so nurture it with love and patience, and you'll see the blessings that come from it.

Forgiveness is essential for keeping peace and harmony in a family. **Ephesians 4:32** teaches us, *"Be kind and compassionate to one another, forgiving each other, just as in Christ God forgave you."* Mistakes are inevitable because no family is perfect, but choosing to forgive instead of holding onto anger helps heal relationships. Forgiveness brings comfort to the heart and restores trust within the family. Letting go of resentment not only helps the person who forgives but also brings peace to the entire household. It creates a space where love can grow, and God's grace can shine brightly.

Forgiveness is a powerful way to strengthen family bonds. When family members choose forgiveness over hatred, they show kindness and understanding, building a home filled with peace and joy. Holding grudges can hurt relationships and cause unnecessary pain, but forgiveness opens the door to healing and fresh starts. **Colossians 3:13** reminds us, *"Bear with each other and forgive one another if any of you has a grievance against someone. Forgive as the Lord forgave you."* With forgiveness, a family becomes stronger, kinder, and more united—a place where everyone feels loved and supported. Forgiveness is the key to turning mistakes into opportunities for growth and making your home a reflection of God's love.

Commit to making your home a playful, pleasant, and purposeful space. Trust God for direction and think positively about your family's future. Speak kindly about your home, spend quality time with your family, and take on your role in building a strong and loving environment. Remember, God has given you your family for a reason, and with His guidance, you can make your home beautiful and blessed. Take ownership of your role, and trust that your efforts will bring lasting joy and peace to your home and everyone in it.

Own Your Home

1. Thank

The first step to treasuring your home is to thank God for it. Gratitude is the foundation of a joyful heart and a peaceful home. Sometimes, it's easy to focus on what we don't have or what we think is missing, but God calls us to look at the blessings He has already given us. **1 Thessalonians 5:18** reminds us, *"Give thanks in all circumstances; for this is God ' s will for you in Christ Jesus.*" No matter the condition or challenges in your home, being thankful shifts your perspective and allows you to see your home as a gift from God.

When we thank God for our home, we acknowledge that it is a space He has chosen for us to grow and thrive. Gratitude doesn't just benefit us; it impacts those around us. When you express thankfulness for your home and family, you inspire others to appreciate their blessings too. By focusing on gratitude, you set the tone for a home filled with joy, peace, and contentment. Make it a habit to thank God daily for your home and to express gratitude to family members for the love and support they provide. This attitude of gratitude will strengthen the bonds within your home.

2. Think Right

How you think about your home shapes your experience of it. Your thoughts influence your feelings and actions, so it's important to think positively and speak life into your home. **Philippians 4:8** says, *"Whatever is true, whatever is noble, whatever is right, whatever is pure, whatever is lovely, whatever is admirable—if* *anything is excellent or praiseworthy—think about such things."* Instead of dwelling on imperfections or comparing your home to others, focus on its uniqueness and the joy it brings.

Thinking positively about your home also means believing in its potential for growth and improvement. Ask God to help you see your home as He does—a place of love, learning, and purpose. When you think right about your home, you create an atmosphere where hope and unity can thrive. Encourage others in your family to do the same, building a shared vision of joy and faithfulness within your home.

3. Talk Nicely

The words you speak about your home and family matter deeply. **Proverbs 18:21** says, *"The tongue has the power of life and death, and those who love it will eat its fruit."* Speaking kindly and respectfully about your home shows that you value and treasure it. Even in moments of frustration, choose words that uplift and encourage. Avoid negative or harsh language that can hurt your family or bring discouragement.

Talking nicely also extends to how you speak about your home to others. When you speak with pride and gratitude about your home and family, you reflect God's goodness and grace. Let your words build up your home and bring peace to your relationships. A home filled with loving communication becomes a sanctuary of harmony and understanding for everyone who lives there.

4. Treasure It

To treasure your home is to treat it with love and respect. **Matthew 6:21** says, *"For where your treasure is, there your heart will be also."* When you treasure your home, you dedicate your time and energy to making it a special place. This means taking care of your physical space—keeping it clean, welcoming, and orderly—and also nurturing the relationships within it. Acts of care and thoughtfulness demonstrate how much you value your home.

Treasure your home by cherishing the moments you share with your family. Every meal, conversation, and laugh is a reminder of God's blessing in bringing you together. When you hold your home close to your heart, you reflect God's love for the people He has placed in your life. Treasure your home as a sacred space where love, faith, and joy can grow abundantly.

5. Trust

Trust is a vital part of treasuring your home. First and foremost, trust God to guide and provide for your home. **Proverbs 3:5-6** says, *"Trust in the Lord with all your heart and lean not on your own understanding; in all your ways submit to him, and he will make your paths straight."* When you place your trust in God, you acknowledge that He is the ultimate foundation of your home and that His plans are perfect.

Trust also means having faith in your family members and their intentions. While no one is perfect, choosing to trust each other builds a sense of security and belonging. Trust fosters open communication, forgiveness, and unity, which are essential to a happy home. Trusting God and one another strengthens the bonds in your family and creates a home where everyone feels safe and loved.

6. Tend

Taking care of your home means looking after it in three important ways: physically, emotionally, and spiritually. **Galatians**

6:9 says, *"Let us not become weary in doing good, for at the proper time we will reap a harvest if we do not give up."* Physically tending to your home means keeping it clean, organized, and beautiful. Cleaning the house, fixing broken items, and decorating are small ways to show gratitude for what God has given you. A tidy and well-kept home creates a welcoming space where everyone feels comfortable and cared for.

Tending to your home emotionally means building strong relationships with the people who live there. Spend time together, encourage one another, and show kindness in your words and actions. **Proverbs 16:24** reminds us, *"Gracious words are a honeycomb, sweet to the soul and healing to the bones."* This means the way you treat your family affects their happiness. Doing small things like sharing meals, laughing together, or saying thank you can make your home a place full of love and peace. When family members feel supported and valued, the home becomes a safe and happy place.

Lastly, tending to your home spiritually is about keeping God at the center of everything. Pray together as a family, read the Bible, and trust Him in your daily life. **Psalm 127:1** says, *"Unless the Lord builds the house, the builders labor in vain."* When a home is built on faith and love for God, it becomes a place of strength and purpose. Spiritual care also helps family members grow closer to one another. Taking care of your home in these three ways makes it flourish, bringing blessings to everyone inside.

3

BE YOUR BROTHER AND
SISTER'S KEEPER

Being your brother and sister's keeper means taking care of the people around you, including your family, friends, and community. It is about taking responsibility for their well-being and showing that you care. This concept comes from the Bible, in **Genesis 4:9,** where Cain asks God, *"Am I my brother's keeper?"* This question teaches us that we should care for one another. Being your brother and sister's keeper means treating others with kindness, compassion, and love. It is about being there for someone when they need help and making a positive impact in their lives. This responsibility is not limited to those we are close to but extends to everyone we meet. In a world that can sometimes feel unkind, being a caring and supportive person helps create a better environment for everyone.

To truly live as your brother and sister's keeper, you must act with love and generosity every day. God has blessed you so that you can be a blessing to others. When you share your time, resources, and kindness, you help bring joy and hope to people's lives. It does not require grand gestures; simple actions like helping a neighbor, offering a kind word, or even smiling at someone can make a big difference. The Bible reminds us in **Galatians 6:10** to *"do good to all people, especially to those who belong to the family of believers."* Each day is a new opportunity to show kindness and demonstrate God's love. Living this way not only helps others but also fills your own heart with joy and peace.

Another important aspect of being your brother and sister's keeper is building strong and meaningful relationships. God created us to live in connection with others. Life is not meant to be lived alone. **Ecclesiastes 4:9-10** tells us, *"Two are better than one because they have a good return for their labor: If either of them falls down, one can help the other up."* This passage reminds us that supporting each other strengthens everyone. By investing time and effort into building relationships, you create an environment where love, trust, and encouragement can grow. It is through these relationships that we truly become keepers of one another.

As a representative of Christ on Earth, you are called to be a shining light in the lives of others. You are an agent of change, and your actions can inspire others to be better. Jesus teaches us to live in love, to speak with love, and to act with love. **Matthew 5:16** says, *"Let your light shine before others, that they may see your good deeds and glorify your Father in heaven."* When you show love and kindness, you bring hope and positivity into the world. Your example can encourage others to embrace a life of compassion and caring, making the world a brighter and more loving place.

Being your brother and sister's keeper means recognizing the value of every person. Everyone deserves to feel loved, important, and appreciated. It is your responsibility to make sure the people around you feel cared for and supported. God has placed people in your life so that you can make their lives better. Some may expect the best without being ready to give their best, but your role is to lift them up and encourage them to grow. Remember, you need people, and people need you. Your presence should bring encouragement, hope, and happiness. By living with love and kindness, you create a ripple effect that touches the lives of many, helping to build a community rooted in harmony and compassion.

The Best Way to Be Your Brother's Keeper.

As your brother and sister's keeper, embracing these qualities can transform lives and inspire others. Here is an extended explanation of each point with an inspirational tone:

1. Love

Love is the foundation of being a brother and sister's keeper. God teaches us in **1 Corinthians 13:13** that the greatest of all virtues is love. To love others means to genuinely care for their happiness, their struggles, and their growth. Love goes beyond words—it is shown through actions that uplift and comfort others. As followers of Christ, our love must be unconditional, just as God's love for us is.

When we love others, we become agents of God's grace, touching lives with kindness and compassion. Simple acts like sharing our time, offering a helping hand, or forgiving those who hurt us demonstrate love in action. Love has the power to heal wounds and build bridges of understanding.

Moreover, love is not only about giving but also about receiving. By showing love to others, we invite them to experience God's love through us. Let your love be genuine and let it transform the lives of those around you, creating a ripple effect of joy and peace.

2. Listen

Listening is one of the most powerful ways to care for those around you. God calls us in **James 1:19** to *"be quick to listen and slow to speak,"* reminding us how important it is to truly hear others. When you listen with an open and loving heart, you show people that they matter. Your attention and presence let them know their words have meaning, and they are not alone in their struggles. Listening builds a bridge of connection, helping you understand their needs, emotions, and experiences more deeply. It is a way of showing God's love through your actions and providing the comfort and care that every person longs for.

Active listening is about more than just hearing words. It means focusing fully on the person, asking thoughtful questions, and showing genuine interest in what they share. When you listen in this way, you become an instrument of God's peace and guidance. Your willingness to truly listen creates a safe space where others feel free to share their burdens, knowing they will be met with compassion and understanding. Let your ears be a channel for God's healing, and let His wisdom guide your responses. By listening with love, you fulfill your role as a brother or sister's keeper, bringing comfort and encouragement to their lives.

3. Lift

To lift others means to help them rise above their challenges and fears. As God's children, we are called to bear one another's burdens (**Galatians 6:2**) and encourage those around us. When someone feels defeated, offering words of hope or extending support can help them find their strength again.

Lifting others might involve physical support, emotional encouragement, or spiritual guidance. Whether it's helping a friend through a difficult time, praying with them, or cheering them on in their goals, you become a source of strength and inspiration.

Remember that when you lift others, you also lift yourself. Helping someone overcome their struggles fills your heart with God's joy and brings light to your own path.

4. Lead

Leadership is about guiding others toward what is good and true. God has given each of us the ability to influence people in a positive way. Being a leader is not about being in charge or having control— it is about being an example of Christ's love, kindness, and honesty. When you lead with integrity, you show others the values that God wants us to live by. Leadership starts with small actions, like helping someone, being fair, or standing up for what is right. These actions show others how to follow God's path.

To lead others, you first need to live a life that reflects God's teachings. When people see your kindness, faith, and humility, they feel inspired to follow your example. A true leader is not proud or selfish but serves with love and care. Jesus Himself showed us this by serving others and putting their needs above His own. You can be a leader by showing compassion, listening to others, and encouraging them to do their best. Your actions can guide people closer to God and give them hope.

As you lead, always seek God's guidance in what you do. Trust Him to give you the wisdom and strength to make the right choices. **Proverbs 3:5-6** tells us to *"Trust in the Lord with all your heart and lean not on your own understanding."* This means putting your faith in God and letting Him direct your steps. Let your life be an example of His love and teachings. When you lead others toward Him, you become a light that helps people see God's grace and goodness.

5. Lighten Lives

God calls us to be the light of the world, as written in **Matthew 5:14:** *"You are the light of the world."* To lighten lives means to bring joy, hope, and peace wherever you go, reflecting the love of God in your actions. Simple gestures like saying a kind word, offering a thoughtful act, or just being a comforting presence can brighten someone's day and remind them of God's care for them. These moments of light show others they are loved, important, and never alone. By sharing God's love in this way, you become a source of encouragement and inspiration for everyone around you.

When you work to lighten lives, you help others see beyond their difficulties and struggles. Your positivity and encouragement can lift their spirits and give them the strength to keep moving forward. With each kind act, you remind them to trust in God's plan and His promises. Every single day is an opportunity to bring peace and joy into someone's heart, whether it's through a smile, a prayer, or helping carry their burdens. Let your light shine brightly in everything you do, and allow God to use you as a beacon of hope and love for those around you. You can make the world a better place by being a reflection of His grace and goodness.

6. Lessen Stress

As your brother and sister's keeper, you have the power to ease the burdens of those around you. Life is often filled with challenges that can feel overwhelming, but God calls us to be His instruments of comfort and relief. Stress can weigh heavily on people's hearts, and even simple acts of kindness can make a big difference. Whether you offer thoughtful advice, lend a helping hand, or simply spend time with someone, your support shows that they are valued and cared for. By being there for others, you reflect God's love and bring hope into their lives.

God invites us to cast all our worries and burdens on Him because He cares for us deeply, as written in **1 Peter 5:7:** *"Cast all your anxiety on Him because He cares for you."* As you help others deal with stress, remind them of this beautiful promise. Encourage them to trust in God as their refuge and strength. By sharing His comforting words, you give others the opportunity to find peace in His presence and lean on His unfailing love.

Kindness and understanding are powerful tools in lessening stress. When you offer a listening ear or show empathy to someone struggling, you remind them that they are not alone. Through your actions, you demonstrate the heart of God—loving, patient, and compassionate. Your presence can bring calm to someone overwhelmed by life's challenges, giving them a sense of reassurance and peace.

Let your role as a keeper be a source of light and encouragement to those who feel burdened. Your ability to help and support is a gift from God, and using it to bless others creates a ripple effect of love and care. Through your kindness and God's strength, you can ease stress and lift the spirits of those around you, making their burdens lighter and their lives brighter.

7. Laugh and Smile

Laughter and a warm smile are precious gifts from God that can lift the spirits of those around us. **Proverbs 17:22** reminds us, *"A cheerful heart is good medicine."* In a family, moments of laughter can bring healing and joy during difficult times. Sharing laughter breaks tension, lightens heavy hearts, and strengthens the bond between family members. Even in challenging situations, laughter reminds us to focus on the blessings in life and to cherish the love we have in our homes. A warm smile adds to this joy, showing kindness and love to those we care about.

Laughter and smiles break down barriers and help people connect more deeply. Smiling at someone lets them know you see them and care about them, even when words fail. It's a small gesture, but its impact is powerful, brightening someone's day and fostering positive relationships. As a family, we are called to be each other's keepers, showing love and compassion whenever we can. **Luke 6:31** encourages us, *"Do to others as you would have them do to you."* By spreading joy through laughter and smiles, we fulfill our calling to bring goodness into the lives of those we love.

Let laughter and smiles be daily reminders of God's love and grace. Every laugh shared and every smile given reflects His goodness in our lives. These small expressions of joy create an atmosphere of positivity and hope, both in the family and beyond. Share laughter and smiles freely, knowing they have the power to transform your home into a place of love and light. By choosing joy, you can inspire and uplift everyone around you, leaving a lasting impact on their hearts and minds.

8. Link

To link with others means to create meaningful connections that strengthen relationships and bring people closer together. God designed us to live in community, and **Ecclesiastes 4:9-10** teaches us, *"Two are better than one because they have a good return for their labor: If either of them falls down, one can help the other up."* Building strong relationships takes effort and a true desire to care for others. Spending time with people, listening to them, and supporting them in times of need helps create a network of love and trust. These bonds remind us that we are never alone and that together we are stronger.

When we link with others, our connections should be rooted in love and faith. Showing kindness and compassion reflects God's design for humanity and brings His blessings to our relationships. **Proverbs 27:17 says,** *"As iron sharpens iron, so one person sharpens another."* By encouraging and uplifting those around us, we can inspire growth and create a community filled with understanding and care. Let God guide your connections, and you will see how they lead to peace, joy, and lasting friendships that honor His purpose for your life.

9. Look After

Looking after others is an essential part of being your brother's and sister's keeper. God calls us to care for those in need and to be His hands and feet on Earth. This involves being attentive to the needs of others and taking action to help them.

Whether it's checking on a neighbor, helping a friend, or supporting a family member, looking after others shows God's love in practice. It demonstrates that you value their well-being and are willing to serve.

Let your care be consistent and genuine, and let God use you to bless others through your acts of compassion.

10. Let Go

Letting go is an act of forgiveness and releasing the heavy burdens we carry in our hearts. God calls us to forgive others, just as He forgives us, as written in **Matthew 6:14-15:** *"For if you forgive other people when they sin against you, your heavenly Father will also forgive you."* When you hold on to anger or resentment, it builds a barrier that prevents you from loving others freely. Forgiveness helps us let go of the pain and bitterness, making room for God's peace to fill our lives. It is a gift you give to yourself and to others.

When we let go of grudges and negativity, we experience a freedom that allows us to live fully in God's joy and peace. Carrying hurt and anger is like holding onto a weight that pulls you down. By letting go, you release that weight and give yourself the chance to heal. Relationships, too, can grow stronger when forgiveness takes the place of resentment. Letting go brings a fresh start, reminding us of the power of God's love to restore and renew.

Letting go is not only about forgiving others—it's also about trusting God with the things you cannot control. Life is full of challenges that can overwhelm us, but God invites us to surrender our worries to Him. He promises to carry our burdens and give us rest **(Matthew 11:28-30).** Trusting God means letting go of the need to have all the answers and instead relying on His wisdom and love. This brings hope and peace to even the most difficult situations.

Letting go means walking in faith and choosing to live with a heart that is free from fear and bitterness. When you let go, you make space for God's blessings to flow into your life. You also set an example of love and grace that others can follow. Let God's love guide you as you release your burdens, and let forgiveness and trust bring peace to your soul. In doing so, you reflect the beauty of God's grace and become a blessing to those around you.

4

RESOLVE CONFLICTS

onflict at home is something that every family faces, and it is important to understand that no home is perfect. Every home is made up of people who have their own struggles, stresses, and shortcomings. Some may feel worried, weak, or even wounded. These emotions can sometimes lead to misunderstandings and tension. However, God calls us to seek peace and live with love in our hearts. **Romans 12:18** reminds us, *"If it is possible, as far as it depends on you, live at peace with everyone."* It is our responsibility to strive for peace and settle differences in a loving way. A peaceful home doesn't mean there is never conflict, but it means there is a commitment to resolving issues with patience and care.

Improving your home takes time, effort, and dedication. Creating a happy and loving home is not something that happens overnight—it requires consistent hard work. It is easy to feel discouraged when problems arise, but do not give up. God is with you, giving you the strength to make your home a better place. **Ephesians 4:2** encourages us to be *"completely humble and gentle;*

be patient, bearing with one another in love." Be willing to forgive, to try again, and to work together to overcome challenges. Even small steps, such as showing kindness and speaking with love, can make a significant difference over time.

Disagreements will happen in every home, but it is how we handle them that defines the atmosphere of the house. Avoid letting disagreements turn into anger, hatred, or hostility. Instead, sit together as a family and talk about the problem. Listen to one another's concerns and try to find a solution that works for everyone. The Bible teaches us in **Matthew 5:9**, *"Blessed are the peacemakers, for they will be called children of God."* When you make an effort to resolve conflicts peacefully, you bring blessings and harmony into your home.

It is also important to identify the things that can cause conflict in your home and work to address or avoid them. Many homes face challenges like communication breakdowns, financial struggles, unrealistic role expectations, or external stress. Knowing these potential sources of conflict helps you prepare to handle them better. Take the time to understand each family member's perspective and needs. Open communication, prayer, and support can prevent small issues from growing into major problems. As a family, make rules for how you will handle disagreements and resolve them in a way that pleases God.

We must also remember that the enemy seeks to steal, kill, and destroy, and the family is one of his targets **(John 10:10).** Be aware of the things that can harm your home and stay vigilant. Pray for God's protection and guidance over your family. Building a happy home is about staying united in love and faith. When you face challenges together and lean on God's strength, your family can overcome even the most difficult situations. Stand strong in His promises and let His love guide you in all that you do.

Finally, enjoy your home and cherish your family. A happy home is built on love, forgiveness, and a commitment to work through problems together. When you seek peace, show kindness, and put God at the center of your home, it becomes a place of joy and comfort. Celebrate the small victories and the love you share as a family. By handling conflicts with wisdom and care, you create a home that reflects God's grace and becomes a blessing to everyone who enters. With God's help, your home can be a place of hope, healing, and happiness.

SOURCE OF CONFLICTS

1. Misunderstanding

Misunderstandings happen when people fail to understand each other's words or intentions. This often leads to confusion, arguments, or hurt feelings. Sometimes, misunderstandings are caused by poor communication or assumptions. In families, these moments are common because everyone has different ways of expressing themselves. God teaches us in **Proverbs 4:7,** *"The beginning of wisdom is this: Get wisdom. Though it cost all you have, get understanding. "* This reminds us to make an effort to understand one another.

To resolve misunderstandings, take time to listen carefully and ask questions if you are unsure of what someone means. Be patient and open-minded in conversations. Prayer can also help us approach situations with a kind and understanding heart. A calm attitude can make it easier to clear up confusion.

Finally, remember the power of forgiveness. If a misunderstanding has caused pain, let go of any resentment. **Ephesians 4:32** tells us to *"Be kind to one another, tenderhearted, forgiving one another, as God in Christ forgave you."* Forgiveness brings healing and restores peace in relationships.

2. Mismanagement

Mismanagement of time, money, or responsibilities is a major cause of tension in families. When chores are unfinished, bills pile up, or plans are disorganized, it creates stress and arguments. God encourages us to be good managers of what we are given. **Luke 16:10 says,** *"Whoever can be trusted with very little can also be trusted with much."*

To address mismanagement, create clear plans and share responsibilities among family members. A weekly schedule or budget can bring order and clarity to the household. Prayer for God's wisdom in managing resources can also guide families in the right direction. Remember to show grace when things don't go as planned. No one is perfect, and mistakes are part of life. Being understanding toward one another helps the family work better as a team.

3. Malice

Malice arises when someone holds onto feelings of anger, jealousy, or resentment and acts in ways that can hurt others emotionally. This behavior damages relationships and disrupts the peace in a home. God warns us against malice in **Ephesians 4:31,** saying, *"Let all bitterness and wrath and anger and clamor and slander be put away from you, along with all malice."* Holding onto these negative emotions prevents love, trust, and harmony from flourishing. A home filled with malice becomes a place of tension and pain rather than comfort and joy. It is important to recognize and address these feelings before they create lasting damage.

To resolve malice, forgiveness is the key. Choose to forgive rather than seek revenge, even when it feels difficult. God calls us to forgive just as He forgives us. Begin by praying for His help to cleanse your heart of bitterness and replace it with love. Honest and kind conversations are also important in resolving malice. Talk to your family members about any misunderstandings or hurt feelings, and approach these discussions with humility and compassion. Clear communication can pave the way for healing and reconciliation, creating a space for love to take root again.

Replace malice with positive actions. **Romans 12:21** teaches us, *"Do not be overcome by evil, but overcome evil with good. "* Show kindness instead of harshness, and choose to act with love even when it feels undeserved. Small gestures of care, like a kind word or a thoughtful action, can help rebuild trust and bring joy back into your home. When you let go of malice and focus on doing good, your home becomes a reflection of God's love and peace, a place where everyone can feel valued and cared for. Let God guide your steps as you work to restore harmony, remembering that His love is greater than any conflict.

4. Mood

Bad mood can create problems at home. When someone feels stressed, tired, or frustrated, they might say things harshly or react in ways that hurt others. This can quickly lead to arguments or cause tension between family members. God reminds us to control our emotions and show gentleness to others. In **Proverbs 15:1,** the

Bible says, *"A gentle answer turns away wrath, but a harsh word stirs up anger."* If we respond to others with kindness, even when we feel upset, it can stop arguments from starting and keep peace in the home.

To handle conflicts caused by bad moods, it helps to first recognize when emotions are running high. Take a moment to breathe and calm yourself before reacting. It's also important to talk openly about how you feel. Share your emotions with your family and let them know what's troubling you. Together, you can pray and ask God for peace and patience to guide your hearts. Open communication allows family members to understand each other better and stops small issues from turning into big problems.

Be patient and offer support when someone in your family is having a bad day. Instead of reacting negatively, show understanding and care. **Colossians 3:13** encourages us to *"Bear with each other and forgive one another."* When you choose forgiveness and kindness, it prevents conflicts from growing and brings harmony back into your home. With God's guidance, you can create a loving and peaceful environment, even when emotions are strong.

5. Mistakes

Mistakes are a natural part of life. No one is immune to them, no matter how wise, careful, or well-intentioned we may be. The Bible makes this clear in **Ecclesiastes 7:20:** *"Indeed, there is no one on earth who is righteous, no one who does what is right and never sins."* This verse reminds us that perfection is not the goal—grace is. When we accept that everyone falls short at times, we become more compassionate and less judgmental toward others.

However, the way we respond to mistakes can either build bridges or create barriers. Criticism, blame, and harsh words often lead to resentment and emotional distance. When someone feels attacked for their failure, they may shut down or pull away. Relationships suffer when mistakes are met with condemnation instead of care. That's why it's so important to choose our words wisely and respond with love, not anger.

Forgiveness and understanding are powerful tools for healing. When we forgive, we release the burden of bitterness and open the door to restoration. Understanding allows us to see the heart behind the mistake and respond with empathy. These responses don't erase the error, but they transform it into an opportunity for growth. In families, friendships, and communities, forgiveness builds trust and strengthens bonds.

Instead of focusing on who's to blame, we should focus on what can be learned. Mistakes can teach us valuable lessons if we're willing to reflect and grow. Working together to find solutions creates unity and shows maturity. Asking questions like "What went wrong?" and "How can we do better next time?" shifts the conversation from conflict to collaboration. When we seek God's wisdom, we gain clarity and direction for moving forward.

Even when we fall repeatedly, God gives us the strength to rise again. **Proverbs 24:16 says,** *"For though the righteous fall seven times, they rise again."* This verse is a powerful reminder that failure is not final. With God's help, we can recover, rebuild, and rise stronger than before. Mistakes don't define us—they refine us. They shape our character and deepen our dependence on God's grace.

In the end, mistakes can become moments of transformation. Families that face failure together and choose forgiveness over frustration grow closer and stronger. Relationships rooted in grace can weather any storm. When we handle mistakes with humility, hope, and healing, we reflect the heart of God—and we create a culture where love triumphs over judgment.

6. Misbehavior

Misbehavior, such as disrespect or dishonesty, can cause tension and conflict within a family. It can hurt trust and create an unhealthy atmosphere where family members feel disconnected. **Proverbs 22:6** reminds us, *"Start children off on the way they should go, and even when they are old they will not turn from it."* This means that teaching good behavior is essential in family life. By guiding children and other family members toward kindness, honesty, and respect, the home can become a place of peace and understanding, where relationships are strengthened instead of harmed.

When addressing misbehavior, it is important to use loving discipline and set clear boundaries. Rather than reacting with anger, take time to calmly explain why the behavior is hurtful and why it needs to change. **Ephesians 6:4** advises parents, *"Do not exasperate your children; instead, bring them up in the training and instruction of the Lord."* By setting expectations in a kind yet firm manner, you can create a framework that encourages positive behavior. Additionally, praying for wisdom and guidance helps to approach the situation with grace and love.

The most powerful way to teach good behavior is to lead by example. Show integrity and kindness in your own actions, as this inspires others in the family to follow. **Colossians 3:12** says, *"Clothe* *yourselves with compassion, kindness, humility, gentleness, and patience."* When family members see you practicing these values, they are more likely to adopt them as well. Positive behavior builds trust and harmony, helping to create a loving and peaceful home where everyone feels valued and respected.

7. Manipulation

Manipulation happens when someone tries to control others in a dishonest or unfair way. It may look like kindness or concern, but deep down, it's about getting what they want without respecting others. This behavior can slowly destroy trust and respect in any relationship. When people feel used or tricked, they begin to pull away and protect themselves. **Proverbs 12:22** says, *"The Lord detests lying lips, but He delights in people who are trustworthy."* God values truth and honesty, and He wants us to treat each other with fairness and love.

To stop manipulation, we must be honest and brave. That means talking clearly about what's happening and how it makes us feel. It's difficult, but it's necessary. We also need to set strong boundaries—rules that protect our hearts and minds. These boundaries help us stay safe and remind others to treat us with respect. Most importantly, we should pray and ask God for wisdom. He can guide us to speak with grace and strength, and help restore honesty where it's been lost.

8. Misuse

Misusing resources, time, or relationships can lead to stress and conflict within a family. For example, wasting money or neglecting responsibilities can create tension and disrupt peace at home. God calls us to be faithful in managing what we have. **Luke 16:10** reminds us, *'Whoever can be trusted with very little can also be* *trusted with much."* This means we should take care of all that God has given us, no matter how small it may seem. When resources are misused, it's important to acknowledge the problem and work together as a family to make things right.

To prevent misuse, families can set clear goals and guidelines for handling resources wisely. This includes budgeting money carefully, using time effectively, and respecting each other's needs. Working together as a team and involving everyone in decision-making builds unity and helps prioritize what truly matters. Prayer can also guide families in using their resources in ways that honor God. Finally, practicing gratitude for what you have teaches responsibility and contentment. Gratitude reduces unnecessary conflicts and creates a peaceful atmosphere where every blessing is valued and used wisely.

9 Money

Money is one of the most common causes of stress in families. It can lead to arguments about how to spend, save, or share resources. When people feel pressure or fear about finances, it can affect their peace and unity. But God calls us to trust Him for our daily needs and to be wise in how we manage what He provides. **Proverbs 21:5** says, *"The plans of the diligent lead to profit as surely as haste leads to poverty."* This verse reminds us that careful planning and patience bring blessings, while rushing and poor decisions can lead to loss.

To handle money problems in a healthy way, families need to talk openly and honestly. Discuss your financial goals, needs, and concerns together. Create a simple budget that everyone agrees on, and stick to it. Don't let money become a secret or a source of fear. Instead, pray together and ask God to guide your decisions. He is faithful to provide, even in hard times. Trusting Him brings peace and helps you avoid stress and confusion.

It's also important to remember that relationships matter more than riches. Money should never be more important than love, respect, and unity in the home. **1 Timothy 6:10** warns us, *"For the love of money is the root of all evil."* When money becomes the main focus, it can lead to selfishness, greed, and division. But when families choose faith over fear and love over lack, they build a strong foundation that lasts.

In the end, peace in the home comes from putting God first and working together with wisdom and love. Money will always be part of life, but it doesn't have to control your heart or your home. With prayer, planning, and patience, families can overcome financial stress and grow stronger in faith and unity.

5

MANAGE YOUR CONFLICTS

1. Agree

Resolving conflict begins with finding common ground. The Bible teaches us in **Amos 3:3,** *"Do two walk together unless they have agreed to do so? "* When family members agree on certain things, it opens the door to peace and mutual understanding. Even in the middle of disagreements, take time to look for areas where you can agree. These may be shared values, goals, or your love for one another. Agreement doesn't mean ignoring differences—it means focusing on unity and working together.

To reach an agreement, listen patiently and calmly to what others have to say. Ask yourself, "What are the things we both want?" By identifying shared intentions, the conflict becomes less about winning and more about improving the situation. Prayer is also powerful during this step. Ask God to guide your heart and thoughts to find unity.

Finally, use agreement as a stepping stone to restore peace. Once you've agreed on key points, build on them to resolve the issue. **Romans 12:18** says, *"If it is possible, as far as it depends on you, live at peace with everyone."* Let agreement be the foundation of reconciliation.

2. Access

Access means taking a step back and examining the situation with a clear mind and heart. It's about understanding the cause of the conflict and its impact on everyone involved. Proverbs 18:13 warns, "To answer before listening—that is folly and shame." Before rushing to conclusions, take time to assess the problem and listen to all sides.

During this stage, ask questions like, "Why are we disagreeing? What is the real issue here?" Understanding the root cause can make resolution easier. When emotions run high, invite God's guidance. Pray for wisdom to see the problem clearly. **James 1:5** promises, *"If any of you lacks wisdom, you should ask God, who gives generously to all."*

Lastly, use what you've learned to address the conflict effectively. Accessing the situation helps you avoid repeating mistakes and equips you to work toward solutions. Let this step bring clarity and peace to your home.

3. Acknowledge

Acknowledging means admitting the feelings, concerns, and perspectives of everyone involved. It's an important step in making others feel heard and valued. **Galatians 6:2** encourages us to *"Carry each other's burdens, and in this way you will fulfill the* *law of Christ. "* By acknowledging each other's struggles, you create an atmosphere of support and love.

Begin by affirming what others feel and think. Say things like, "I understand why you're upset," or "I see how this affects you." This simple act can ease tension and pave the way for resolution. Remember, acknowledgment does not mean agreeing with everything—it means showing empathy and respect.

Finally, let acknowledgment build stronger family bonds. When people feel understood, they are more willing to find solutions together. Acknowledgment lays the groundwork for forgiveness and reconciliation.

4. Apologize

Apologies are powerful tools for resolving conflicts. Saying "I'm sorry" when you've hurt someone shows humility and opens the door to healing. **Colossians 3:13** reminds us, *"Bear with each other and forgive one another if any of you has a grievance against someone. Forgive as the Lord forgave you. "* An apology should come from the heart and express true regret for your actions.

When apologizing, be specific. Say what you are sorry for and acknowledge the impact of your actions. For example, "I'm sorry for raising my voice—it wasn't kind." This helps rebuild trust and shows sincerity. Pray for God's strength to overcome pride and apologize fully.

Finally, use apologies as steps toward making things right. They create an opportunity for forgiveness and restoration. A genuine apology can transform relationships and bring peace into your home.

5. Ask

Asking for help or clarification is an essential step in resolving conflicts. It shows humility and a willingness to listen. **Matthew 7:7** says, *"Ask and it will be given to you; seek and you will find; knock and the door will be opened to you."* Asking can help you understand the other person's perspective and find solutions together.

Start by asking gentle, respectful questions. For example, "How can we fix this together?" or "What do you think we can do to improve things?" Avoid blaming or accusing—it's about working together, not against each other.

Lastly, use asking as a way to invite God's wisdom into the situation. Pray and seek guidance to handle the conflict in a way that honors Him. Asking brings clarity and builds cooperation within the family.

6. Answer with Love and Respect

How you respond in a conflict can make all the difference. God calls us to answer with love and respect, even when emotions run high. **Proverbs 15:1** teaches, *"A gentle answer turns away wrath, but a harsh word stirs up anger."* Choosing words wisely can prevent the situation from escalating.

When you answer, be kind and avoid sarcasm or anger. Speak truthfully but lovingly, showing the other person that you value their feelings. Before responding, take a moment to pray for calmness and wisdom in your words.

Finally, let your answers reflect God's love. **Ephesians 4:29** says, *"Do not let any unwholesome talk come out of your mouths, but* *only what is helpful for building others up. "* Use your words to build peace and strengthen relationships.

7. Amend

Amending involves making changes and taking action to resolve the issue. It's about moving forward and finding ways to prevent conflicts from happening again. **Romans 12:9** encourages us to *"Hate what is evil; cling to what is good. "* Making amends means choosing good actions and attitudes to restore peace.

Start by identifying what needs to change. Ask, "How can we avoid this problem in the future?" Work together to create solutions that benefit everyone. Small changes, like better communication or setting boundaries, can make a big difference.

Finally, take steps to rebuild trust and harmony. Amending requires consistency and effort, but it creates lasting peace. With God's guidance, amending becomes an opportunity for growth and unity.

8. Avoid

Avoiding unnecessary conflicts is a proactive way to keep peace in the home. While some disagreements are natural, others can be prevented through wise choices. **Proverbs 20:3** says, *"It is to one's honor to avoid strife, but every fool is quick to quarrel. "* Avoiding conflict doesn't mean ignoring problems—it means being thoughtful about how you approach situations.

To avoid conflicts, create clear boundaries and rules for respectful communication. Pray together as a family for patience and understanding. Be mindful of words and actions that might hurt others or escalate tension.

Lastly, make a daily effort to foster peace and love in your home. Avoiding conflict helps create a harmonious environment where everyone feels valued. Let God's wisdom guide your decisions, bringing joy and unity into your family.

6

HOW TO MAKE EACH
MEMBER FEEL IMPORTANT

Every person longs to be seen, heard, and valued. In a family or community, making each member feel important is not just a kind gesture—it's a godly responsibility. **Romans 12:10** encourages us to *"Be devoted to one another in love. Honor one another above yourselves."* When we honor others, we reflect the heart of God and build a home where love, respect, and unity flourish. This chapter will explore simple, intentional ways to affirm each person's worth, strengthen relationships, and create an atmosphere where everyone feels cherished and included

1. Compliment

Giving compliments is a simple but powerful way to make someone feel loved and appreciated. Compliments show that you notice and value the good qualities in others. In **Proverbs 16:24**, the Bible says, *"Gracious words are a honeycomb, sweet to the soul and healing to the bones. "* Words of praise can uplift spirits and remind people of their worth. Complimenting someone can be as simple as acknowledging their hard work, kindness, or talents.

To build a home where compliments are common, be intentional about looking for opportunities to appreciate others. When your child does well in school, tell them, "I'm proud of your hard work." When your spouse prepares a meal, say, "This is delicious. Thank you for your effort." These words strengthen relationships and bring warmth to your home. Pray for God to give you a heart that sees the best in others.

Finally, remember that compliments should always be sincere. Empty praise can feel meaningless, but genuine words of encouragement have the power to heal and inspire. When you make it a habit to compliment others, you help create a home where everyone feels valued and loved.

2. Congratulate

Congratulating others on their achievements is a way of sharing in their joy and making them feel important. **Romans 12:15** tells us, *"Rejoice with those who rejoice."* Celebrating someone's success, whether big or small, shows that you care about their happiness and recognize their efforts. This practice strengthens bonds and fosters a spirit of unity in the home.

Take time to acknowledge milestones and accomplishments, such as birthdays, graduations, or even small victories like completing a task. Say things like, "I'm so happy for you," or "Well done, you worked so hard for this!" These moments of shared joy remind each person in the home that their efforts are seen and celebrated.

Lastly, let your congratulations be heartfelt and genuine. By rejoicing with your family and friends, you build a culture of love and encouragement. Your home becomes a place where every achievement is treasured, and everyone feels supported.

3. Celebrate

Celebrations are sacred moments that bring families together and create lasting memories. They are opportunities to rejoice, reflect, and reconnect. **Ecclesiastes 3:4** reminds us, *"There is a time to weep and a time to laugh, a time to mourn and a time to dance."* Every celebration is a gift—a time to laugh, love, and lift one another up. Whether it's a birthday, anniversary, or personal milestone, these moments help us appreciate God's goodness and the people He has placed in our lives.

At every celebration, begin by inviting God into the moment. He is the source of joy, unity, and healing. Start with prayer, thanking Him for the grace to gather and the gift of life. Praise Him for giving you a time to celebrate, and ask that His presence fills the atmosphere with peace and purpose. Let your words be gentle, your actions thoughtful, and your mind focused on love. Speak with grace, act with compassion, and think with humility. A celebration should be a safe space where everyone feels valued, respected, and welcomed.

Use celebrations as a time to strengthen relationships, reconcile differences, and bring healing to hurting hearts. Pray that the gathering will draw your family closer, mend broken bonds, and offer comfort to those in pain. Let laughter be medicine and love be the message. Ask God to protect the gathering from conflict or crisis, and to turn every moment into a memory of peace and praise.

Whether it's a birthday, anniversary, or personal milestone, make it meaningful. Include everyone in the planning so they feel involved and important. Even small gestures—a shared meal, a kind word, a warm hug—can leave a lasting impact. A joyful home is one where God is honored, love is abundant, and every person is cherished. When you celebrate together, you declare that life is worth rejoicing, relationships are worth restoring, and God is worthy of praise.

Even small gestures—a shared meal, a kind word, a warm hug—can leave a lasting impact. Include everyone in the planning so they feel involved and important. End the celebration with prayer, thanking God for the joy experienced and the unity built. A joyful home is one where God is honored, love is abundant, and every person is cherished. When you celebrate together, you declare that life is worth rejoicing, relationships are worth restoring, and God is worthy of praise.

4. Consider

Considering others means putting their needs and feelings before your own. **Philippians 2:3-4** says, *"Do nothing out of selfish ambition or vain conceit. Rather, in humility, value others above yourselves, not looking to your own interests but each of you to the interests of the others. "* This attitude of humility and care shows people that they matter.

Start by taking small steps, like asking how someone is feeling or offering to help with a task. When someone in your family feels stressed, take the time to listen and support them. Show them that their well-being is important to you.

Lastly, make consideration a daily practice. When every member of the home acts with kindness and care, it creates a loving environment where everyone feels respected and loved. Your home becomes a reflection of God's love and grace.

5. Cherish

To cherish someone is to hold them dear and treat them with great care. **Ephesians 5:29** says, *"After all, no one ever hated their own body, but they feed and care for their body, just as Christ does the church."* This teaches us to care for others as we care for ourselves, with love and attention.

Show your family that you cherish them through your actions. Spend quality time together, give them your full attention, and express your love daily. Say things like, "You mean so much to me," or "I'm thankful to have you in my life." These words and actions remind them of their value.

Finally, let cherishing others be a way of life. When you treasure the people in your home, you create an atmosphere of love and gratitude. Your home becomes a haven where everyone feels safe and appreciated.

6. Connect and Commit

Building strong connections in the home is essential for a happy family. **Ecclesiastes 4:9-10** says, *"Two are better than one because they have a good return for their labor: If either of them falls down, one can help the other up."* Connection means being present for one another and creating bonds of trust and love.

Take time to connect with each person in your home. Share meals, have meaningful conversations, and pray together as a family. Show commitment by prioritizing your relationships and being dependable. When someone feels loved and connected, they know they belong.

SYAVIHA MULENGYA

Finally, use connection to strengthen your home's foundation. A connected family is one where everyone feels supported and valued. Let God guide your relationships, bringing unity and peace to your home.

7. Communicate

Clear and loving communication is key to resolving conflicts and building strong relationships. **Proverbs 18:21** reminds us that *"The tongue has the power of life and death. "* Words can either hurt or heal, so use them wisely to express love and understanding.

Start by creating an open environment where everyone feels safe to share their thoughts and feelings. Listen without interrupting and respond with kindness. When misunderstandings arise, talk them through with patience and respect.

Finally, use communication to build each other up. **Ephesians 4:29** teaches us to speak only what is helpful for building others. Let your words bring life, hope, and encouragement to your family. A home with open and loving communication is one filled with peace and harmony.

8. Correct in Love

Correction is necessary, but it should always be done with love and care. **Proverbs 3:12** says, *"For the Lord disciplines those he loves, as a father the son he delights in. "* Correction is not about punishing but about guiding others toward what is right.

When correcting someone, do it gently and with understanding. Avoid harsh words that may hurt or discourage them. Instead, explain your concerns and offer solutions. Pray for wisdom to address the situation in a way that brings healing and growth.

Corrections strengthen your relationships rather than weaken them. When done in love, correction shows that you care deeply for the person's well-being. It creates an environment where everyone can grow and thrive together in love and faith.

7

BROKEN BONDS, SILENT STORMS

Many families struggle with unhappiness because of things like poor communication, lack of respect, selfish behavior, and unresolved problems. When love fades and people stop listening to each other, pain and frustration grow. The Bible reminds us in **Amos 3:3**, *"Can two walk together, unless they are agreed?"* Peace in the home begins when family members choose unity, understanding, and kindness over conflict and pride.

God wants families to be places of joy, love, and support—not stress and sorrow. That's why it's important to deal with problems early and with wisdom. **Proverbs 15:1** says, *"A gentle answer turns away wrath, but a harsh word stirs up anger."* When we speak with love and listen with care, we create a home where healing can happen and happiness can grow. This chapter will help you discover the causes of unhappiness and how to restore peace through God's truth and grace.

1. Betray

Betrayal is one of the most painful things that can break a family. When trust is broken, whether through dishonesty, infidelity, or any other act of disloyalty, it damages relationships deeply. Trust is the foundation of any family, and when it is betrayed, it brings hurt, anger, and disappointment. **Proverbs 12:22** says, *"The Lord detests lying lips, but He delights in people who are trustworthy."* Honesty is key to building and keeping trust within the home.

To heal from betrayal, family members must be willing to forgive and rebuild trust. This takes time and effort, but with God's guidance, healing is possible. Pray together as a family and ask God for wisdom and strength to move forward. Communication is also important—be open about feelings and work toward understanding each other's perspectives.

Finally, take steps to prevent betrayal in the future. Commit to honesty and loyalty in all your relationships. Show love and respect for one another, and let God's grace guide you. **Ephesians 4:32** reminds us, *"Be kind and compassionate to one another, forgiving each other, just as in Christ God forgave you."* With love and forgiveness, families can overcome betrayal and grow stronger.

2. Bitterness

Bitterness grows when people hold onto anger, hurt, or resentment. It can quietly destroy relationships within a family, making the home a place of tension instead of peace. **Hebrews 12:15** warns us, *"See to it that no one falls short of the grace of God and that no bitter root grows up to cause trouble and defile many."* Bitterness poisons hearts and spreads negativity.

To overcome bitterness, begin by acknowledging it and seeking God's help to release it. Pray for a heart filled with love and forgiveness. Talk openly about the issues causing bitterness and work together to resolve them. Holding onto past wrongs will only cause more harm, but forgiveness can bring freedom and healing.

Finally, replace bitterness with kindness and understanding. Choose to focus on the good in each other instead of dwelling on mistakes. **Colossians 3:13** says, *"Bear with each other and forgive one another."* When families practice forgiveness and compassion, the home becomes a place of love and joy.

3. Blame

Blaming others for problems creates division in a family. When people point fingers instead of working together to solve issues, it leads to anger and defensiveness. **Matthew 7:3** reminds us, *"Why do you look at the speck of sawdust in your brother's eye and pay no attention to the plank in your own eye?"* Blame often blinds us to our own faults and keeps us from finding solutions.

To stop the cycle of blame, focus on taking responsibility for your own actions. Instead of accusing others, work together to understand the problem and find ways to fix it. Pray as a family for unity and wisdom, and ask God to help you approach conflicts with humility.

Lastly, replace blame with encouragement. Speak words that build others up instead of tearing them down. **Ephesians 4:29** says, *"Do not let any unwholesome talk come out of your mouths, but only what is helpful for building others up."* When families support one another instead of blaming, they create a stronger bond.

4. Battle

Constant fighting or arguing can tear a family apart. Disagreements are natural, but when they turn into constant battles, they create a toxic atmosphere. **James 1:19** advises, *"Everyone should be quick to listen, slow to speak, and slow to become angry."* Listening and understanding are essential to resolving conflicts peacefully.

To reduce battles, set clear rules for resolving disagreements. Encourage calm discussions where everyone has a chance to share their feelings. Pray for patience and ask God to guide your words and actions. Remember, the goal is not to win an argument but to restore peace in the home.

Focus on creating harmony in the family. Choose love over anger and work together to build a peaceful home. **Proverbs 15:1** reminds us, *"A gentle answer turns away wrath, but a harsh word stirs up anger."* With God's help, families can overcome battles and grow closer.

5. Bias

Bias or favoritism within a family can cause feelings of rejection and hurt. When one person is favored over another, it creates jealousy and tension. **James 2:1** warns, *"My brothers and sisters, believers in our glorious Lord Jesus Christ must not show favoritism."* Treating everyone equally is key to maintaining harmony in the home.

To overcome bias, make an effort to show love and appreciation to every family member. Acknowledge each person's unique qualities and celebrate their strengths. Pray as a family for unity and fairness, and ask God to help you see each person with His eyes of love.

Build an atmosphere of acceptance and respect. Let every family member feel valued and important. **Colossians 3:14** says, *"And over all these virtues put on love, which binds them all together in perfect unity. "* When families treat each other with fairness and love, they grow stronger together.

6. Breakdown

A breakdown in communication or understanding can create distance in a family. When people stop talking or listening to each other, it leads to frustration and isolation. **Proverbs 18:13** says, *"To answer before listening—that is folly and shame. "* Listening is an important part of maintaining strong relationships.

To fix communication breakdowns, encourage open and honest conversations. Create a safe space where everyone feels comfortable sharing their thoughts and feelings. Pray together as a family for wisdom and understanding, and ask God to strengthen your bonds.

Make communication a daily habit. Spend time talking, sharing, and listening to one another. **Ephesians 4:15** encourages us to *"speak the truth in love. "* When families communicate with love and respect, they build stronger connections and avoid misunderstandings.

7. Boasting

Boasting or pride can create tension and hurt feelings within a family. When someone constantly seeks attention or belittles others, it creates a sense of inequality. **Proverbs 27:2** says, *"Let someone else praise you, and not your own mouth; an outsider, and* *not your own lips. "* Humility is essential to maintaining peace and respect in the home.

To prevent boasting, focus on encouraging and uplifting others instead of seeking praise for yourself. Celebrate each family member's achievements and show genuine interest in their lives. Pray for humility and ask God to help you treat others with kindness and respect.

Finally, practice gratitude and thankfulness. Recognize that all blessings come from God, and give Him the glory for your accomplishments. **1 Thessalonians 5:18** says, *"Give thanks in all circumstances. "* When families live with humility and gratitude, they create a loving and supportive environment

8

BUILT TO LAST: FOUNDATIONS OF A GODLY HOME

A strong home is built on love, trust, and godly wisdom. It's not just about having a roof over your head—it's about creating a place where hearts feel safe, valued, and connected. The Bible says in **Proverbs 24:3 − 4**, *"By wisdom a house is built, and through understanding it is established; through knowledge its rooms are filled with rare and beautiful treasures."* This means that a strong home grows through wise choices, kind words, and shared understanding.

When family members pray together, forgive quickly, and support each other, the home becomes a place of peace and joy. Respect, honesty, and patience help build strong relationships. God's Word gives us the tools to create homes that reflect His love. A strong home is not perfect—but it is full of grace, truth, and unity.

The Heart of the Home: Love, Faith, and Unity

1. Respect

Respect is the heartbeat of a healthy and joyful home. It means recognizing the value of each person, regardless of age or role, and treating them with kindness, dignity, and care. When we honor one another, we create a space where love can flourish and wounds can heal. **Romans 12:10** reminds us, *"Be devoted to one another in love. Honor one another above yourselves."* This verse calls us to elevate others, not just tolerate them. Respect is not earned through perfection—it is given because every person is made in the image of God.

Practicing respect begins with how we speak and listen. Listening without interrupting, responding with gentleness, and avoiding harsh or hurtful words are powerful ways to show honor. Even in moments of disagreement, respect allows us to disagree without destroying each other. It also means recognizing personal boundaries—giving space when needed, and showing empathy when someone is hurting. Respect is not weakness; it is strength under control. Prayer helps us cultivate this spirit, softening our hearts and guiding our words.

Respect must be modeled before it can be multiplied. Parents who respect their children teach them to respect others. Spouses who honor each other build a culture of love and trust. Children who see respect in action will carry it into their friendships, schools, and future homes. A respectful home is a peaceful home—where voices are heard, hearts are healed, and relationships are strengthened. When respect reigns, joy follows, and the home becomes a sanctuary of grace.

2. Responsibility: Building a Home That Works Together

Responsibility is the glue that holds a family together. It means doing your part, fulfilling your duties, and being accountable for your actions. **Galatians 6:5** says, *"For each one should carry their own load."* This verse reminds us that everyone has a role to play. Whether it's cleaning, caring, or contributing, responsibility shows maturity and builds trust. A responsible person doesn't wait to be told—they take initiative and serve with a willing heart.

In a responsible home, everyone works together. Parents lead by example—teaching time management, stewardship, and consistency. Children learn to contribute by doing chores, caring for their belongings, and helping others. These small acts build character and prepare them for life beyond the home. Responsibility also means owning up to mistakes and making things right. It's not about being perfect—it's about being faithful. Prayer helps each family member stay focused and committed to their role.

Consistency is the key to responsibility. When each person does their part regularly, the home becomes a place of order and peace. No one feels overwhelmed, and everyone feels valued. Responsibility creates pride in one's work and joy in shared success. It strengthens bonds and builds a legacy of trust. A responsible home is not just functional—it's fruitful. It becomes a place where love is shown through action, and every member feels empowered to make a difference.

3. Reliability

Reliability means being someone your family can count on. It involves keeping your promises, being dependable, and standing by your loved ones during tough times. **Proverbs 20:6** says, *"Many claim to have unfailing love, but a faithful person who can find? "*

Faithfulness and reliability are essential for building trust and stability in the home.

To show reliability, follow through on your commitments, whether it's small promises like helping with homework or big ones like being there in difficult moments. Being reliable shows your family that they can always lean on you for support and love.

Finally, let your reliability reflect God's faithfulness. Be a source of encouragement, reminding your family that just as they can depend on you, they can always depend on God. A reliable family member brings comfort and strength to the home.

4. Reconciliation

Reconciliation is the process of making peace after conflict. Every family faces disagreements, but healing begins when we choose forgiveness over resentment. The Bible encourages us in **Colossians 3:13**, *"Bear with each other and forgive one another if any of you has a grievance against someone. Forgive as the Lord forgave you."* Forgiveness is not just a feeling—it's a decision to release the hurt and rebuild the relationship. When we reconcile, we restore love, trust, and unity in the home.

The journey toward reconciliation starts with humility. Admitting mistakes, asking for forgiveness, and listening with an open heart are powerful steps. Prayer plays a vital role—inviting God to heal wounds and soften hearts. When family members come together in prayer, it creates space for grace and understanding. Reconciliation is not about winning an argument; it's about winning back the relationship. It requires patience, empathy, and a commitment to peace.

Make reconciliation a daily habit. Don't let anger linger or bitterness take root. **Ephesians 4:26** warns, *"Do not let the sun go down while you are still angry."* This means we should seek peace quickly and not allow conflict to fester. A home that practices reconciliation becomes a refuge of love—a place where mistakes are forgiven, hearts are mended, and joy is restored. When reconciliation is embraced, families grow stronger, and God's presence fills the home with harmony.

5. Reward

Rewarding family members for their efforts, kindness, or achievements shows appreciation and encourages positivity. Even small gestures like saying "thank you" or giving a hug can make a big difference. **Proverbs 11:25** says, *"A generous person will prosper; whoever refreshes others will be refreshed."* Rewarding others spreads joy and strengthens relationships.

Celebrate achievements in your family, no matter how big or small. A good grade, a completed chore, or a kind act deserves recognition. Rewards don't always have to be material; they can be simple things like praise, quality time, or a fun activity together.

Lastly, let rewards remind your family of God's blessings. When you reward others, you show them they are valued and loved, making your home a happier place.

6. Recognition

Recognition means letting your family know that their efforts and contributions matter. It's about appreciating each person's unique qualities and celebrating their strengths. **Romans 12:6** reminds us, *"We have different gifts, according to the grace given* *to each of us.* " Recognizing each other builds confidence and strengthens the family bond.

Take time to notice the little things family members do to help or show love. Acknowledge their efforts with kind words like, "I'm proud of you," or "You're doing a great job." Recognition encourages family members to continue doing good.

Lastly, pray for a heart that sees and appreciates the good in others. When everyone feels recognized, the home becomes a place of love, support, and joy.

7. Reassurance

Reassurance is about reminding your family that they are loved and not alone. Life can be stressful, but knowing that someone cares makes all the difference. **Isaiah 41:10** says, *"Do not fear, for I am with you; do not be dismayed, for I am your God.* " Reassuring your family reflects God's unwavering love and comfort.

Comfort your family during tough times with kind words and actions. Let them know that you are there for them and that God is, too. Simple gestures like a hug or a smile can reassure them of your love.

Lastly, make reassurance a daily practice. Remind your family often that they are valuable and loved. Reassurance strengthens bonds and brings peace to your home.

In every value—*Respect, Responsibility, Reliability, Reconciliation, Rewards, Recognition,* and *Reassurance*—we must turn to God for guidance. These principles are powerful, but they become transformational when rooted in prayer and scripture. God is the ultimate source of wisdom, love, and strength. When we seek Him daily, He equips us to build a home that reflects His grace.

SYAVIHA MULENGYA

Proverbs 3:5-6 reminds us, *"Trust in the Lord with all your heart and lean not on your own understanding; in all your ways submit to him, and he will make your paths straight."* A God-centered home is a guided home.

Prayer is the lifeline of a strong family. It invites God into every conversation, every challenge, and every celebration. When families pray together, they grow together. Prayer softens hearts, heals wounds, and strengthens bonds. It reminds us that we are not alone in our efforts—God walks with us. Whether you're asking for patience, peace, or provision, God hears and answers. Make prayer a daily habit, and let it shape your words, actions, and attitudes.

When God's love is at the center, your home becomes more than just a place to live—it becomes a place of joy, peace, and purpose. It reflects heaven on earth. The family becomes a team, a ministry, and a testimony of God's goodness. Challenges may come, but with God's presence, you'll overcome them with grace. Let your home be a light to others—a place where love is spoken, forgiveness is practiced, and hope is alive. With God as your foundation, your family will flourish and your legacy will shine.

9

HOW TO MAKE YOUR
HOME PEACEFUL

1. Patient

B eing patient is one of the most important ways to make a home peaceful. Patience means waiting calmly, even in situations that are frustrating or difficult. In families, there are often disagreements or misunderstandings, but patience allows you to respond with love instead of anger. The Bible says in **Proverbs 15:18,** *"A hot-tempered person stirs up conflict, but the one who is patient calms a quarrel."* Patience helps to calm tension and keep peace in your home.

To practice patience, remind yourself that everyone makes mistakes and has struggles. Be willing to give others time to grow and learn. When children or loved ones fail to meet expectations, respond with kindness instead of harshness. Pray for patience, asking God to help you stay calm and compassionate in difficult situations.

Make patience a habit. Practice being patient even in small things, like waiting your turn to speak or understanding someone's point of view. With patience, you create a home filled with forgiveness and love, where everyone feels respected and valued.

2. Present

Being present means giving your family your full attention and spending quality time with them. In a peaceful home, family members don't feel ignored or left out; they feel seen and appreciated. **Ecclesiastes 3:1** reminds us, *"There is a time for everything, and a season for every activity under the heavens. "* This means there's a time to focus on your family and be with them fully.

To be present, put away distractions like phones or TV when you're spending time with loved ones. Listen when someone speaks, and show that their thoughts and feelings are important to you. Moments of presence, whether during meals, prayers, or conversations, strengthen your family's bond.

Finally, make being present part of your daily routine. Share simple joys like laughing together, playing games, or helping with tasks. Your presence creates a home filled with connection and love, making your family healthy and happy.

3. Positive

Being positive means focusing on the good and choosing an attitude of hope and encouragement. In families, negativity can lead to hurt feelings and conflicts, but positivity inspires everyone to keep going. **Philippians 4:8** encourages us, *"Whatever is true, whatever is noble, whatever is right, whatever is pure, whatever is* *lovely—think about such things."* Positivity reflects God's goodness and brings joy to your home.

To be positive, speak words of encouragement and kindness. When challenges arise, remind your family that God is with you and His plans are good. Avoid complaining or criticizing, and instead look for solutions and blessings.

Lastly, let your positivity be contagious. When you choose to see the best in every situation, your family feels inspired to do the same. Positivity builds a strong and hopeful home where love and joy shine.

4. Pleasant

Being pleasant means creating a friendly and welcoming atmosphere in your home. Pleasantness involves kindness, respect, and a cheerful attitude that makes others feel comfortable and loved. **Proverbs 16:24** says, *"Gracious words are a honeycomb, sweet to the soul and healing to the bones."* Pleasantness brings healing and harmony to your family.

To be pleasant, greet your family with smiles and kind words every day. Avoid harsh or critical comments, and instead show gratitude and appreciation for each person. A pleasant home is one where everyone feels safe and valued.

Finally, let pleasantness become a way of life. Choose kindness and gentleness in all your interactions. A pleasant attitude creates a happy and peaceful environment that brings joy to everyone in the home.

5. Prayerful

A prayerful home is a peaceful home. Praying together as a family strengthens your bond and invites God's presence into your home. **Philippians 4:6-7** reminds us, *"Do not be anxious about anything, but in every situation, by prayer and petition, with thanksgiving, present your requests to God. And the peace of God ··· will guard your hearts and your minds in Christ Jesus."* Prayer brings comfort and hope in difficult times.

Start each day with family prayers, thanking God for His blessings and asking for His guidance. Pray for your loved ones and their needs, and encourage everyone to trust in God's plan. Prayer helps to calm worries and reminds your family that they are never alone.

Finally, make prayer a foundation of your family life. Pray together during meals, before bedtime, and in times of joy or challenges. A prayerful home is one where God's peace and love fill every corner, making your family strong and hopeful.

6. Problem Solver

Being a problem solver means working together to find solutions instead of dwelling on conflicts. Families face challenges, but when you approach them with wisdom and love, you can overcome them. **Proverbs 3:5-6** reminds us, *"Trust in the Lord with all your heart and lean not on your own understanding; in all your ways submit to Him, and He will make your paths straight."*

To solve problems, listen to each other's concerns and think about solutions that benefit everyone. Avoid blaming or arguing, and instead work as a team. Seek God's guidance in finding answers, and pray for wisdom and peace.

Lastly, celebrate every step toward resolution. Solving problems strengthens your family's trust and makes your home happier and healthier. When everyone feels supported, your home becomes a place of hope and love.

7. Polite

Being polite means treating others with respect and consideration. Politeness helps to prevent conflicts and shows your family that you care about their feelings. **Colossians 4:6** says, *"Let your conversation be always full of grace."* Politeness reflects God's kindness and brings harmony to your home.

To be polite, say "please," "thank you," and "sorry" often. Show courtesy in your words and actions, such as listening without interrupting or helping when needed. Politeness creates an environment of mutual respect.

Finally, let politeness set the tone for your family interactions. Practice politeness daily, and teach your children to be considerate of others. A polite home is one where everyone feels valued and loved.

8. Proactive

Being proactive means taking action to prevent problems and create positive change in your home. It's about looking ahead and preparing for challenges instead of waiting for things to go wrong. **Proverbs 22:3** says, *"The prudent see danger and take refuge."* Being proactive helps keep your family safe and peaceful.

To be proactive, plan ahead and create routines that support your family's well-being. Communicate openly, and address concerns before they become bigger issues. Ask God for wisdom to guide your actions.

Finally, let your proactive attitude inspire your family. When you actively work to improve your home, you create an atmosphere of security and joy. Proactivity keeps your family healthy, hopeful, and strong.

9. Pure of Heart

Having a pure heart means living with honesty, love, and kindness. A pure heart creates peace in your home and reflects God's grace. **Matthew 5:8** says, *"Blessed are the pure in heart, for they will see God. "* Purity of heart helps you to focus on what is right and good.

To cultivate a pure heart, choose honesty in your words and actions. Avoid negative thoughts or behaviors, and seek God's guidance to stay on His path. Be kind and compassionate, treating each family member with love and care.

Let purity of heart shine in your family. A home filled with God's love and truth brings happiness and peace. Your family becomes a reflection of God's goodness, inspiring others and bringing hope to those around you.

10

BE THE CHANGE YOU
WANT TO SEE

Happy in Public and horrible in Private

In a small town, there was a teacher whom everyone admired. She was known for her wisdom, kindness, and hopeful attitude. Students loved her so much that they nicknamed her "The Best Mum." Her classroom was full of laughter, inspiration, and growth. She encouraged her students to dream big, guiding them patiently and creating an atmosphere of positivity. The entire community praised her as a role model and often awarded her for being an exceptional teacher. However, this admiration masked a sad reality—the teacher was not the same kind and loving person at home.

At home, her own children felt like strangers to their mother. Every time she came home, they avoided her as much as possible. She didn't enjoy talking with them or building a bond. Instead, she believed that her children were always wrong and deserved punishment, never admitting any faults of her own. Her harshness led to endless arguments, and whenever her children tried to correct her behavior, she would yell, creating chaos and unrest in the household for days or even weeks. The children grew tired of the lack of peace, and some eventually chose to live with their uncle to escape the harsh environment.

The situation was heartbreaking, especially when her children faced the confusion of how others saw their mother. At school, her students would say, "You're so lucky! You have the best and kindest mum. I wish my mum were like yours!" But her children would respond, "Who are you talking about? That's not our mum—maybe it's someone else you're describing." They could not understand how their mother could be so loving at school but so cold at home. Though she was celebrated publicly, her own children felt disconnected from her, as if she were two completely different people.

Her public recognition reached its peak when she received an award for being the kindest teacher. One of her children, overwhelmed with frustration, wrote a letter to the school. The letter asked, "Why do you give an award for kindness when she's so mean? Ask us, her children, and we will tell you." This letter caught the attention of the headteacher, who decided to confront the teacher about her behavior. She was shocked and embarrassed to learn how her actions had affected her family. For the first time, she faced the reality of her shortcomings, realizing she had failed as a mother. The teacher returned some of her awards, acknowledging that she did not deserve them, and vowed to make a change.

From that moment, the teacher began to reflect deeply on her life and behavior. She turned her focus to improving her relationship with her children. With humility and effort, she worked to rebuild the trust and love she had lost. Slowly but surely, peace and joy returned to her home. Her children began to feel valued and cared for, and the house transformed into a place of harmony and happiness. The teacher's story reminds us that true greatness lies not in public admiration but in how we treat those closest to us. Her journey of self-reflection and growth shows that it is never too late to make positive changes, especially when it comes to family.

Live what You Preach

Matthew 7:5 teaches us to reflect on ourselves before judging others: *"First remove the plank from your own eye, and then you will see clearly to remove the speck from your brother's eye."* This reminds us not to blame others without first addressing our own weaknesses. In a family, it is important to understand that no one is perfect. Each member matters greatly, and we all share responsibility in creating a loving and peaceful environment. Start by evaluating your own actions, correcting mistakes, and striving to become a better person. When we commit to doing what is right, we become peacemakers, as encouraged in **Matthew 5:9**: "Blessed are the peacemakers, for they shall be called sons of God."

Gaining the admiration of outsiders means little if we are not kind and respectful to our family at home. As **Proverbs 14:1** reminds us, *"The wise woman builds her house, but the foolish pulls it down with her hands."* This teaches us to be builders of love, unity, and peace in our families. For a family to thrive, we need to cultivate good character, strong commitment, open communication, and genuine collaboration. Reflect daily on your actions and ask yourself, "Am I building my family or tearing it down?" Even though no family is perfect, we can rely on **Philippians 4:13:** *"I can do all things through Christ who strengthens me,"* to help us overcome our struggles and improve ourselves.

Genesis 4:9 reminds us to care for each other when Cain asks, *"Am I my brother's keeper?"* Yes, we are our brother's keeper. Each of us has a role in uplifting our family and making them proud. **Proverbs 22:6** says, *"Train up a child in the way he should go, and when he is old he will not depart from it."* This verse highlights the importance of upholding family values and morals. Good manners and discipline begin at home, shaping our future and ensuring we live in harmony with others. Without this foundation, as **Proverbs 10:17** warns, *"He who keeps instruction is in the way of life, but he who refuses correction goes astray,"* we risk straying into unhappiness and conflict.

Although change can be difficult, **2 Corinthians 5:17** offers hope: *"Therefore, if anyone is in Christ, he is a new creation; old things have passed away; behold, all things have become new."* By trusting in God, you can become a better version of yourself. **Galatians 6:7** also reminds us, *"Do not be deceived, God is not mocked; for whatever a man sows, that he will also reap."* Sow seeds of peace, love, respect, and progress within your family to reap the blessings of joy and unity. Regularly reflect on your actions and strive to align them with God's word. When you are at peace with yourself, you can extend that peace to others, strengthening your family.

Your family is the best place to demonstrate your love, commitment, and care. **Hebrews 13:16** teaches us, *"But do not forget to do good and to share, for with such sacrifices God is well pleased."* Let your family be your first priority, where you live out your values and set a good example. Avoid hypocrisy, as Jesus warns in **Matthew 23:28:** *"Even so you also outwardly appear righteous to men, but inside you are full of hypocrisy and lawlessness."* A family is our first church, the foundation for living a godly life. Make your home a place of love and kindness, where everyone feels valued and respected.

Finally, evaluate yourself regularly and work to do good, trusting in God's guidance. **Jeremiah 29:11** reminds us, *"For I know the thoughts that I think toward you, says the Lord, thoughts of peace and not of evil, to give you a future and a hope."* This verse encourages us to rely on God's plan as we strive for positive change. A happy and loving family requires effort and commitment from every member. By sowing seeds of goodness and seeking God's help, we can overcome struggles and become blessings to our families. Let your actions reflect your love for God and your family, building a legacy of faith, love, and harmony. As **Joshua 24:15** states, *"But as for me and my house, we will serve the Lord."* This is the ultimate commitment to creating a home filled with joy and God's presence.

1. Set a Good Example

The Bible tells us in **Matthew 5:16**, *"Let your light so shine before men, that they may see your good works and glorify your Father in heaven."* Setting a good example is one of the most powerful ways to bring positive change to your family. Your actions speak louder than words, and when you live with integrity, kindness, and love, others around you will notice. Being consistent in your behavior, whether at home or outside, shows that you truly value goodness and honesty. Your family looks up to you, so let your life be a reflection of the values you hold dear.

Children and younger members of the family often learn by observing adults. **Proverbs 22:6** says, *"Train up a child in the way he should go, and when he is old he will not depart from it."* This verse reminds us of the importance of being a role model. When you set a good example, you help shape the character of your loved ones. By living with respect, discipline, and humility, you guide your family to grow in the right direction. Always remember, your actions at home have a lasting impact on those who see and learn from you.

2. Show the Way

John 14:6 says, "I am the way, the truth, and the life." Showing the way means leading others with wisdom and truth. In a family, it's important to be a guide and provide clear direction. Whether it's teaching values, sharing knowledge, or helping with decisions, your support is vital in helping others grow. Show your family what it means to live with love, patience, and understanding. When you lead them with these qualities, they will be inspired to follow your example and walk in the path of righteousness.

Psalm 32:8 says, "I will instruct you and teach you in the way you should go; I will guide you with My eye." Leading the way also requires listening to God's word and sharing His wisdom with your family. Encourage your loved ones to trust in the Lord and seek His guidance in everything they do. By showing them how to live a life of faith and purpose, you help your family stay united and strong in their journey together.

3. Speak with Love

Ephesians 4:29 says, *"Let no corrupt word proceed out of your mouth, but what is good for necessary edification, that it may impart grace to the hearers."* Speaking with love is essential in building a happy and peaceful family. Words have incredible power—they can heal or hurt, uplift or tear down. Choose words that encourage and inspire, even in difficult situations. When you speak kindly and thoughtfully, your family feels valued and respected.

Proverbs 15:1 teaches us, *"A soft answer turns away wrath, but a harsh word stirs up anger."* Sometimes conflicts arise, but how you communicate makes all the difference. When you respond with love and gentleness, you create an atmosphere of peace and understanding. Practice speaking with patience and compassion, always aiming to build stronger relationships. Love-filled words strengthen bonds and bring joy to your family.

4. Support Other Family Members

Galatians 6:2 reminds us, *"Bear one another's burdens, and so fulfill the law of Christ."* Supporting your family members during their struggles is an important way to show care and commitment. Whether it's offering help with tasks, listening to their concerns, or praying for them, your support can make a huge difference. Being there for one another fosters trust and unity within the family.

Romans 15:1 says, *"We then who are strong ought to bear with the scruples of the weak, and not to please ourselves."* This verse encourages us to be patient and understanding with those who may be struggling. Show your family that you are willing to help them through their challenges and guide them to overcome obstacles. Your love and support remind them that they are not alone and that together, you can face anything.

5. Solve Any Issue

Matthew 18:15 teaches us, *"If your brother sins against you, go and tell him his fault between you and him alone. If he hears you, you have gained your brother."* Solving issues within the family requires open and honest communication. Avoid blame and approach conflicts with a calm and loving attitude. Sit down with your family members and work together to find solutions that bring peace and understanding.

Proverbs 3:5-6 encourages us to trust in God's guidance: *"Trust in the Lord with all your heart, and lean not on your own understanding; in all your ways acknowledge Him, and He shall direct your paths."* Before addressing problems, pray for wisdom and guidance. With God's help, you can resolve conflicts in a way that strengthens your family and brings harmony. Always seek to mend broken relationships and restore peace.

6. Set Well

1 Corinthians 14:40 says, *"Let all things be done decently and in order."* Setting things well in the family means creating structure and order that allows everyone to thrive. Establish clear rules, routines, and values that help maintain harmony. When the family is organized and each member knows their responsibilities, life runs more smoothly.

Colossians 3:23-24 reminds us, *"And whatever you do, do it heartily, as to the Lord and not to men."* Setting things well also means leading by example with dedication and effort. Whether it's managing household tasks, teaching good habits, or fostering teamwork, do everything with a spirit of love and cooperation. This ensures that the family stays united and strong.

11

THE BEST FOUNDATION FOR
A HAPPY HOME

God is the best foundation for building a strong and lasting home. **Psalm 127:1** declares, *"Unless the Lord builds the house, they labor in vain who build it."* This verse reminds us that without God at the center, a home cannot truly thrive. To build a home that withstands the challenges of life, we must rely on God's guidance and wisdom. A strong foundation rooted in faith is essential to surviving the storms, stress, and situations of the current world. Families are often targeted by practices and influences that promote division and wrong values. These seemingly innocent practices can undermine unity and weaken the bonds within a home. But when God is the cornerstone, amazing things happen—peace, love, and strength fill the home, allowing it to stand firm.

Your home is blessed, and it holds a great mission. **Proverbs 24:3-4** says, *"Through wisdom a house is built, and by understanding it is established; by knowledge the rooms are filled with all precious and pleasant riches."* This verse highlights that your home is not just a physical space but a place where love and wisdom thrive. It is your responsibility to enjoy and excel in your home, knowing that it matters greatly. Your home has the potential to be a blessing not only to your family but also to other families and even the community at large. Whatever you do in your home should bring happiness, joy, and positivity. By nurturing a strong foundation, you honor the blessings God has given you and fulfill your home's purpose as a source of light and love for others.

As the builder of your home, you must ensure it is built with love, unity, and faith. **Matthew 7:24-25** illustrates this beautifully: *"Therefore whoever hears these sayings of Mine, and does them, I will liken him to a wise man who built his house on the rock. And the rain descended, the floods came, and the winds blew and beat on that house; and it did not fall, for it was founded on the rock."* This verse emphasizes the importance of building a home on a strong foundation. A home built on Christ's teachings can withstand life's challenges and emerge stronger. A joyful and peaceful home fosters love and success, ensuring that every member feels valued and supported. Unity and harmony are key, and they can only be achieved when you focus on the foundation of your home.

Protect Your Home

.We must always be careful and watchful about the dangers that can harm our homes. **Ephesians 6:12** reminds us, *"For our struggle is not against flesh and blood, but against the rulers, against the authorities, against the powers of this dark world, and against the spiritual forces of evil in the heavenly realms."* This verse shows us that the challenges we face in protecting our homes are not just physical but also spiritual. There are hidden influences and forces working against the unity of families, aiming to cause harm and division. It is important to understand that these forces do not come in obvious ways. Instead, they often appear through practices or ideas that seem harmless but, over time, can weaken the bonds of love and trust within a home.

One example is the growing belief that families no longer need to spend time together or value one another. This can seem like a minor issue, but it slowly creates distance and lack of connection among family members. When time is not set aside to bond, share, and support each other, misunderstandings and conflict can grow. Some practices even promote wrong values that destroy the importance of family unity and togetherness. These can include placing material success above relationships, encouraging selfishness, or neglecting the need for forgiveness. These actions and attitudes act like cracks in a foundation, and over time, they threaten the stability of the home.

To protect your home from these dangers, it is important to rely on God's guidance and wisdom. Prayer is a powerful way to invite God into your family and strengthen its foundation. When you pray together as a family, you build a bond not only with one another but also with God. **Proverbs 3:5-6** encourages us, *"Trust in the Lord with all your heart and lean not on your own understanding; in all your ways submit to Him, and He will make your paths straight."* By trusting God and staying committed to His word, families can overcome challenges and remain united. Prayer helps to guard your home and create a loving, peaceful atmosphere where everyone feels valued and cared for.

Keeping God as the foundation of your home ensures that it stays strong no matter what challenges arise. With God's help, families can reject harmful influences and focus on building love, respect, and trust. When the family follows God's values, it becomes a place of joy, peace, and protection. In **John 16:33**, Jesus says, *"In this world you will have trouble. But take heart! I have overcome the world."* This reminds us that while difficulties may come, God is always there to help us overcome them. A family built on God's love and principles will not only stand firm but will also shine as an example to others. Guard your home with prayer, strong values, and love, knowing that God is the ultimate protector and guide.

PUT GOD FIRST

1. Source

God is the source of everything that creates a happy and healthy home. **James 1:17** says, *"Every good and perfect gift is from above, coming down from the Father of the heavenly lights."* This means that all the blessings we experience in our families—love, peace, joy, and wisdom—come from God. He is the beginning and foundation of everything good in our lives. When we rely on God as the source, we acknowledge that He is the one who gives us the ability to build a loving and united home. His guidance helps us overcome challenges and fills our family with joy.

Families must always remember that God is the center of their purpose. **Acts 17:28** reminds us, *"For in Him we live and move and have our being."* Everything we do in our home—whether it is showing love, teaching values, or spending quality time—should be based on God's word. When families trust Him as the ultimate source, their bonds grow stronger, and they find direction in their relationships. Building a home begins with recognizing God's role in all the blessings we enjoy and using those blessings to nurture love and unity.

2. Supplier

God is the supplier who meets every need of the family. **Philippians 4:19** says, *"And my God will meet all your needs according to the riches of His glory in Christ Jesus."* This verse assures us that no matter what struggles families face, God is always there to provide for them. He supplies everything from physical needs, such as food and shelter, to emotional and spiritual needs, such as peace, hope, and forgiveness. Families can trust in God's endless provision and be confident that He will sustain them through all circumstances.

Not only does God supply material needs, but He also gives wisdom to families to help them make the right decisions. **James 1:5** says, *"If any of you lacks wisdom, you should ask God, who gives generously to all without finding fault, and it will be given to you."* This shows that when families turn to God for help, He supplies the understanding they need to live peacefully and grow together. Families that trust in God's provision experience His blessings and are able to support and love one another deeply.

3. Strength

God is the source of strength for families, giving them the ability to face challenges with courage. **Isaiah 41:10** says, *"Do not fear, for I am with you; do not be dismayed, for I am your God. I will strengthen you and help you; I will uphold you with my righteous right hand."* This verse emphasizes that God's strength is always available when families feel weak or overwhelmed. Relying on His power helps families stay united and overcome trials together.

Strength from God also helps families show patience and kindness during difficulties. **Philippians 4:13** reminds us, *"I can do all things through Christ who strengthens me."* When families encounter misunderstandings or disagreements, God's strength enables them to forgive each other, be patient, and work towards reconciliation. Families that rely on God's strength can face life's challenges with love and grace, ensuring a happy and healthy home.

4. Security

God provides security for families, protecting them from harm and danger. **Proverbs 18:10** says, "The name of the Lord is a strong tower; the righteous run to it and are safe." This verse highlights God's role as a refuge and protector for families. Whether it is physical danger or emotional struggles, God's presence gives families a sense of safety and peace. Trusting Him as the ultimate security ensures that the family feels protected and cared for.

Security also includes emotional and spiritual protection. **Psalm 16:8** says, *"I keep my eyes always on the Lord. With Him at my right hand, I will not be shaken."* Families that rely on God find comfort and assurance in His love, even in uncertain times. God's faithfulness creates an environment of safety where family members feel secure and supported. This sense of security strengthens the family and promotes peace and joy.

5. Safety

God ensures the safety of families in every aspect of life. **Psalm 91:4** says, *"He will cover you with His feathers, and under His wings you will find refuge; His faithfulness will be your shield and rampart."* This verse describes God's protective care over families, shielding them from harm and giving them a safe place to grow and thrive. His love provides a sense of comfort and peace that fills the home.

Safety also includes the emotional and spiritual well-being of family members. **Isaiah 26:3** says, *"You will keep in perfect peace those whose minds are steadfast because they trust in You."* Families that place their trust in God experience peace and comfort, free from fear and anxiety. A safe home is one where God's presence is felt and where family members support one another in love and kindness.

6. Satisfaction

God brings satisfaction and fulfillment to families. **Psalm 107:9** says, *"For He satisfies the longing soul and fills the hungry soul with goodness."* This verse shows that God knows the needs and desires of each family member and provides them with joy and contentment. Families that rely on God find happiness in His blessings rather than in worldly pursuits that may lead to emptiness. God's love fills the heart and creates a home filled with joy.

True satisfaction comes from living according to God's teachings. **Matthew 6:33** says, *"But seek first His kingdom and His righteousness, and all these things will be given to you as well."* When families prioritize God's will, they experience lasting happiness and fulfillment. A home centered on God becomes a place of joy, harmony, and gratitude.

7. Stability

God gives stability to families, helping them remain strong and steady in every situation. **Psalm 62:6** says, *"Truly He is my rock and my salvation; He is my fortress; I will not be shaken."* This verse highlights God's role as the foundation that keeps families grounded and united. Stability in a home allows families to face challenges without fear and to grow stronger together.

Stability also comes from God's wisdom and guidance. **Isaiah 33:6** says, *"He will be the sure foundation for your times, a rich store of salvation and wisdom and knowledge."* A stable family relies on God's teachings to navigate relationships, decisions, and challenges. With God's guidance, families remain united and strong, no matter what they face.

8. Strengthen

God strengthens families by helping them grow in love, faith, and unity. **Colossians 2:7** says, *"Rooted and built up in Him, strengthened in the faith as you were taught, and overflowing with thankfulness."* Families that rely on God are continuously strengthened in their relationships and their faith. His love nurtures family members and encourages them to support and care for one another.

Challenges and trials can also be opportunities for God to strengthen families. **James 1:2-3** says, *"Consider it pure joy, my brothers and sisters, whenever you face trials of many kinds, because you know that the testing of your faith produces perseverance."* This verse reminds us that struggles help families rely more on God and grow closer together. Families that trust God experience His strength and are able to build a happy and healthy home filled with love and joy.

God is the foundation of a happy and healthy home. He is the source of love, joy, and every good thing that makes a family strong. He supplies all that a family needs, from physical necessities to spiritual guidance. God gives us strength to overcome difficulties, keeps us secure and safe, and brings peace and satisfaction to our homes. A family rooted in God has stability and can grow in love and unity, no matter the challenges they face. As **Psalm 127:1** says,

"Unless the Lord builds the house, the builders labor in vain." This means that when God is at the center of a home, that home becomes a place of hope, happiness, and harmony.

Christ is the only foundation that can withstand the storms of life. Homes built on Him are protected from division, selfishness, and the negative influences of the world. God's love unites families and helps them experience joy and success. When we trust in Him, He becomes our provider, protector, and guide. He brings safety and peace, creating a home where love grows and everyone is valued. A home founded on God's word will thrive and reflect His blessings, not only to the family but also to the community around them.

Choose God first

Because God is the foundation, we must actively seek His presence in our families. First, **put God first in everything.** Make Him the priority in your home by reading the Bible together, praying together, and following His teachings. When you put God first, He will walk with you and lead your family in the right direction. **Matthew 6:33** reminds us, *"But seek first His kingdom and His righteousness, and all these things will be given to you as well."* When we place God above all else, He provides for our needs and blesses our homes with peace and unity.

Second, **invite God into your home.** Welcome Him into your daily lives by creating a habit of prayer and worship as a family. Pray for His guidance and wisdom as you make decisions. Let Him lead every aspect of your home life, and allow His word to be your guide. Third, **involve God in all you do.** Trust Him with your joys, struggles, and plans. Lean on Him for strength when challenges arise, and give Him thanks for the blessings He provides. **Proverbs 3:5-6** says,

"Trust in the Lord with all your heart and lean not on your own understanding; in all your ways submit to Him, and He will make your paths straight."

Inquire from God. Seek His wisdom in prayer and ask for His direction when you face difficult choices. **James 1:5** says, *"If any of you lacks wisdom, you should ask God, who gives generously to all without finding fault, and it will be given to you."* When you ask God for guidance, He will answer and provide clarity. By involving Him in every area of your life, you allow Him to build your home on His unshakable foundation. A home built on God is strong, secure, and filled with His love and blessings. Let God walk ahead of you and guide you as you strive to build a happy, healthy, and united family.

12

VALUES THAT BRING
HAPPINESS AT HOME

1. Honesty

Honesty is the foundation of trust in any home. **Proverbs 12:22** says, *"The Lord detests lying lips, but He delights in people who are trustworthy."* This verse shows us how much God values honesty. In a family, honesty means being truthful and transparent with one another. When family members are honest, they can rely on each other without fear of deception. It removes doubt and builds strong relationships. Trust grows when family members consistently tell the truth, creating an environment of safety and love. Without honesty, misunderstandings, conflicts, and mistrust can take root, breaking the family bond.

Honesty also plays a vital role in resolving conflicts. When disagreements arise, speaking the truth with kindness can help everyone address the problem and work toward a solution. **Ephesians 4:15** reminds us to *"speak the truth in love."* Being truthful does not mean being harsh; it means expressing your thoughts and feelings in a way that promotes understanding and

SYAVIHA MULENGYA

healing. Families that embrace honesty are better equipped to face challenges together, as honesty fosters open communication and mutual respect. It ensures that conflicts do not create lasting harm but instead lead to growth and reconciliation.

Living with honesty goes beyond speaking the truth; it also includes acting with integrity. **Colossians 3:9** teaches, *"Do not lie to each other, since you have taken off your old self with its practices."* This means being honest in actions as well as words. Parents, in particular, have a responsibility to lead by example. Children learn from what they see, so when parents model honesty and fairness, they teach their children to value these qualities. By living with integrity, each family member contributes to a home where everyone feels respected, valued, and secure.

Honesty strengthens the bonds between family members and creates a home filled with love and trust. It allows everyone to feel safe sharing their thoughts and emotions without fear of judgment or rejection. A family built on honesty becomes a place of peace, where each member knows they are valued for who they truly are. As **Proverbs 11:3** says, *"The integrity of the upright guides them."* By making honesty a priority, families grow closer, build lasting trust, and create a strong and peaceful foundation that honors God and His teachings.

2. Harmony

Harmony is an important rule for creating a peaceful and united home. **Psalm 133:1** says, *"How good and pleasant it is when God 's people live together in unity!"* Harmony in a family means working together and supporting each other. It requires understanding and listening to one another with love and care. A harmonious home is a place where family members value each other's opinions and are willing to compromise to find solutions. They focus on peace rather than arguments or disagreements. This creates an environment where everyone feels respected and loved.

To build harmony in your home, strong communication is key. **Ephesians 4:3** encourages us to *"Make every effort to keep the unity of the Spirit through the bond of peace."* Families that make communication a priority can address problems openly and avoid unnecessary conflicts. When family members take time to listen to each other and express their thoughts with kindness, it strengthens their bond and brings understanding. Strong communication leads to better relationships and makes the home a place of love and joy.

The foundation of harmony is keeping God at the center of your home. When families invite God into their lives, He provides the peace and wisdom they need to live in unity. With God's guidance, families can overcome challenges and stay united during difficult times. A harmonious home built on God's love brings stability, rest, and happiness to everyone. It becomes a place where each family member can thrive and grow in an atmosphere of peace and togetherness.

3. Helpful

Helping one another is a rule that strengthens family relationships. **Galatians 6:2** says, *"Carry each other's burdens, and in this way, you will fulfill the law of Christ."* Helping others shows love and care. In a home, this could mean assisting with chores, listening to each other's problems, or supporting one another during tough times. Being helpful creates a sense of unity and teamwork.

A helpful attitude teaches children important values like compassion and responsibility. **Acts 20:35** says, *"It is more blessed* to give than to receive." Families that make helping one another a priority experience joy and gratitude. They learn to put others before themselves, building a home filled with selflessness and care.

4. Hope

Hope is the anchor of a happy home. **Romans 15:13** says, *"May the God of hope fill you with all joy and peace as you trust in Him."* A hopeful home is one where family members encourage each other and trust that better days are ahead. Hope gives families the strength to face challenges and keeps them united during tough times.

Families can grow hope by leaning on God's promises and praying together. **Jeremiah 29:11** reminds us, *"For I know the plans I have for you, declares the Lord, plans to prosper you and not to harm you, plans to give you a future and a hope."* By trusting in God's plans, families remain optimistic and joyful, even during trials. Hope strengthens the bonds of love, reminding everyone that brighter days are ahead.

5. Hard Work

Hard work is a rule that builds a strong and successful home. **Proverbs 14:23** says, *"All hard work brings a profit, but mere talk leads only to poverty."* A hardworking family puts effort into their goals and responsibilities, whether it's providing for the home, studying, or caring for one another. Hard work shows commitment and dedication to building a better future.

Parents who demonstrate hard work inspire their children to be responsible and diligent. **Colossians 3:23** encourages us, *"Whatever you do, work at it with all your heart, as working for the Lord, not for human masters."* A hardworking family does everything with love and purpose, creating a home where everyone contributes to its success and happiness.

6. Humility

Humility is the foundation of a loving and respectful home. **Philippians 2:3** teaches us, *"Do nothing out of selfish ambition or vain conceit. Rather, in humility value others above yourselves."* This verse reminds us that being humble means putting others first and caring for their needs. In a family, humility creates understanding, as each member works to support and serve one another. It helps people focus on kindness rather than pride. When family members approach situations with humility, they create a peaceful environment where everyone feels valued and respected.

Humility also involves admitting mistakes and seeking forgiveness. **Proverbs 11:2** says, *"When pride comes, then comes disgrace, but with humility comes wisdom."* Families must understand that no one is perfect, and asking for forgiveness is not a sign of weakness but of strength. A humble heart allows family members to learn from their errors and build stronger relationships. When parents show humility, they set a positive example for their children, teaching them the importance of admitting faults and showing respect to others. This creates a cycle of growth and understanding within the home.

A home filled with humility becomes a place of love and unity. Family members become more patient, compassionate, and willing to listen to each other. They recognize that everyone has value and that serving one another brings joy and harmony. **Ephesians 4:2** encourages us to *"Be completely humble and gentle; be patient, bearing with one another in love."* By practicing humility, families build a strong foundation of peace and care, ensuring a happy and healthy home where every member thrives

7. Habits

Good habits are essential for a peaceful and organized home. **Proverbs 22:6** says, *"Start children off on the way they should go, and even when they are old, they will not turn from it."* Habits such as praying together, helping with chores, and spending quality time strengthen family bonds. Teaching children positive habits early ensures they grow with discipline and responsibility.

Habits also bring structure to a home. **Colossians 3:17** says, *"And whatever you do, whether in word or deed, do it all in the name of the Lord Jesus, giving thanks to God the Father through Him."* Families that build habits of gratitude, kindness, and respect create a joyful and peaceful environment. Good habits set the foundation for a strong and happy home.

8. Humor

Laughter is a gift that brings joy to a home. **Proverbs 17:22** says, *"A cheerful heart is good medicine, but a crushed spirit dries up the bones."* Humor creates lighthearted moments and helps families bond through shared joy. A home filled with laughter is a place where love and happiness thrive.

Humor also helps families cope with stress and challenges. **Ecclesiastes 3:4** reminds us there is *"a time to weep and a time to laugh."* Finding moments to share joy, even in difficult times, brings hope and strengthens family relationships. Laughter is a blessing that keeps a home happy and united.

9. Heroism

Heroism is about selflessness and bravery in supporting one another. **John 15:13** says, *"Greater love has no one than this: to lay down one ' s life for one ' s friends."* In a home, heroism means making sacrifices for the well-being of others. It involves standing up for what is right and protecting loved ones.

Everyday heroism teaches children the value of love and responsibility. **Galatians 5:13** says, *"Serve one another humbly in love."* Families that practice heroism inspire loyalty and respect, creating a strong foundation of care and commitment.

10. Hospitality

Hospitality reflects God's love through kindness and generosity. **Hebrews 13:2** says, *"Do not forget to show hospitality to strangers, for by so doing some people have shown hospitality to angels without knowing it."* A hospitable home welcomes guests with warmth and care, creating an atmosphere of love and acceptance.

Hospitality also strengthens family bonds. **Acts 20:35** reminds us, *"It is more blessed to give than to receive."* Sharing meals, opening your home, and helping those in need teach family members the joy of giving. A hospitable home becomes a place of blessing and connection.

11. Honor

Honor is about showing respect and valuing one another. **Exodus 20:12** says, *"Honor your father and your mother, so that you may live long in the land the Lord your God is giving you."* In a home, honor means treating each other with kindness and understanding. Respecting parents, siblings, and children fosters love and trust in the family.

Honor also involves honoring God in everything we do. **1 Corinthians 10:31** says, *"So whether you eat or drink or whatever you do, do it all for the glory of God."* A home that practices honor creates an environment of love, where everyone feels valued and appreciated.

12. Happiness

Happiness is the fruit of a loving and united home. **Psalm 118:24** says, *"This is the day that the Lord has made; let us rejoice and be glad in it."* A happy home is one where family members celebrate God's blessings and find joy in each other. Gratitude and positivity create a joyful and peaceful environment.

Happiness also comes from following God's will. **Proverbs 3:5-6** reminds us to *"Trust in the Lord with all your heart and lean not on your own understanding."* When families trust God, they find peace and happiness, even in challenges. A happy home is one filled with love, laughter, and faith in God.

Family rules are like the foundation of a house; they support and hold everything together. The 12 rules—honesty, harmony, helpfulness, hope, hard work, humility, good habits, humor, heroism, hospitality, honor, and happiness—are essential for creating a loving and peaceful home. Each of these rules is rooted in God's word, guiding families to live with love, respect, and care for one another. These principles create an environment where every family member can thrive, feel valued, and work together for the good of the home. **Proverbs 24:3-4** says, *"By wisdom a house is built, and through understanding it is established; through knowledge, its rooms are filled with rare and beautiful treasures."* Following family rules based on God's teachings brings wisdom, understanding, and countless blessings.

Family rules matter because they teach each member important values that last a lifetime. These rules encourage respect, kindness, and teamwork, which strengthen the bonds between family members. They also help resolve conflicts, promote peace, and ensure that the family remains united, even during challenges. A family that follows God's principles becomes a light to others, showing how His love can transform a home into a place of joy and harmony. **Psalm 127:1** reminds us, *"Unless the Lord builds the house, the builders labor in vain."* By keeping God at the center of these rules, families can build strong, lasting foundations.

To apply these family rules, start by **putting God at the center of your home.** Pray together as a family, read the Bible, and discuss how His teachings can guide your relationships. Inviting God into your home ensures that He is involved in every decision and that His love is the foundation of your actions. **Proverbs 3:6** reminds us, *"In all your ways submit to Him, and He will make your paths straight."* Let God be your source of wisdom and strength as you strive to follow these rules.

Second, **live out these rules with intention.** Honesty, harmony, humility, and all the other principles should be practiced in your daily interactions. Parents should lead by example, showing children what it means to live with love and respect. For instance, speak with kindness, forgive easily, and support each other through challenges. As **Galatians 5:13** says, *"Serve one another humbly in love."* By following these rules, families can create an atmosphere of mutual care and understanding.

Finally, **evaluate and grow as a family.** Take time to reflect on how well your family is applying these rules and where improvements can be made. Encourage open communication so that every member feels heard and valued. Celebrate the successes and small victories of living out these principles, and lean on God for guidance when challenges arise. **Colossians 3:17** reminds us, *"And whatever you do, whether in word or deed, do it all in the name of the Lord Jesus, giving thanks to God the Father through Him."* With God's help and commitment to these family rules, your home can become a place of love, peace, and happiness that blesses everyone within it.

13

FUN FAMILY CREATE JOY
AT HOME

Having fun together as a family is one of the best ways to create joy and strengthen relationships at home. When families play together, they build bonds that bring happiness and a sense of belonging. The Bible reminds us in **Ecclesiastes 3:4,** *"A time to weep and a time to laugh, a time to mourn and a time to dance."* Laughter and joy are essential to a peaceful and loving home. Playing games or participating in fun activities helps family members connect in a positive way. It reminds everyone that the home is a place of love and togetherness, not a place of stress or tension.

When a family plays together, it also helps create peace and teamwork. Fun activities encourage family members to work together and support one another, making them feel like a united team. Having peace with one another brings peace to the entire home. **Colossians 3:13** encourages us, *"Bear with each other and forgive one another if any of you has a grievance against someone."* Playtime strengthens these principles, as family games and activities teach patience, respect, and compromise. It creates an atmosphere where everyone feels comfortable and valued.

Family fun also breaks routines and promotes creativity. Sometimes, daily life can become monotonous, but engaging in fun activities brings excitement and fresh energy to the home. Playing games builds resilience and trust among family members, as they learn to face challenges and celebrate victories together. **Proverbs 17:22** reminds us, *"A cheerful heart is good medicine."* Having a positive atmosphere with laughter and enjoyment helps families stay hopeful and motivated, even during difficult times. It allows each member to feel included and appreciated.

Lastly, family fun contributes to building strong and lasting relationships. Activities such as games, hobbies, and celebrations promote communication and understanding. They help family members open up and share their thoughts and feelings while enjoying each other's company. This strengthens the bond between siblings, parents, and even extended family members. A happy, playful home is not only a blessing to those living in it but also a shining example to others. Making time for fun together shows that you care about your family and value the love you share. Remember, joy and peace at home are gifts that God desires for every family.

BRING THE CELEBRATION HOME

Celebrating at home brings joy, unity, and lasting memories for the entire family. It allows everyone to come together, share happiness, and strengthen the bond between family members. Celebrations create an opportunity to express gratitude for God's blessings, as **Psalm 118:24** reminds us, *"This is the day that the Lord has made; let us rejoice and be glad in it."* Whether it's birthdays, achievements, or small milestones, celebrating at home nurtures a sense of belonging and love. It breaks routines, brings laughter, and helps family members focus on the positive aspects of life. Moreover, celebrations build a warm and happy environment where everyone feels valued and appreciated, fostering peace and harmony in the home. Such joyful moments remind us of the importance of family and the joy that comes from spending time together in love and gratitude.

1. Recreation

Playing games and having fun bring recreation to the family, giving everyone the chance to recharge and enjoy life together. **Ecclesiastes 3:12-13** reminds us, *"I know that there is nothing better for people than to be happy and to do good while they live. That each of them may eat and drink, and find satisfaction in all their toil—this is the gift of God."* Recreation allows family members to take a break from their busy schedules and spend quality time together, strengthening their bond in a joyful way.

Recreation is also important for physical and mental health. Engaging in fun activities, such as sports, board games, or outdoor adventures, brings energy and happiness. It gives families the opportunity to laugh together and enjoy the simple moments in life. **Proverbs 17:22** says, *"A cheerful heart is good medicine,"* reminding us that recreation promotes not only happiness but also good health.

Additionally, recreation fosters creativity and a positive mindset. When families take time to play and relax together, they discover new ways to connect and share joy. Recreation builds memories that last a lifetime and reminds everyone that the home is a place of love and happiness. It is a way to celebrate God's blessings as a family.

2. Reflection

Games and fun activities allow families to reflect on their relationships and experiences. **Psalm 46:10** says, *"Be still, and know that I am God."* This reminds us that reflection is important, and moments of fun often create opportunities to pause and appreciate each other. Through reflection, families can better understand each other's needs, strengths, and values.

Reflection during family playtime helps members identify what makes their home joyful and peaceful. It gives everyone a chance to think about how they can improve communication and teamwork. **Galatians 6:4** says, *"Each one should test their own actions. Then they can take pride in themselves alone, without comparing themselves to someone else."* By reflecting on their actions, family members can grow and strengthen their bonds.

Finally, reflection encourages gratitude. It allows family members to express gratitude to God for the fun times they share and the blessings they enjoy. Gratitude builds a sense of unity and appreciation, reminding everyone that their family is a gift from God. Reflection through play fosters a loving and grateful atmosphere at home.

3. Resolution

Family games can help resolve conflicts and bring family members closer together. **Ephesians 4:26-27** teaches us, *"In your anger do not sin. Do not let the sun go down while you are still angry, and do not give the devil a foothold."* Playful moments often create an environment where tensions can be eased and problems addressed with a lighter heart. Games can encourage open communication and help resolve misunderstandings.

In addition, working as a team during games promotes problem-solving and cooperation. Families learn to rely on one another to achieve goals, building trust and understanding. **Proverbs 15:1** says, *"A gentle answer turns away wrath, but a harsh word stirs up anger."* Games allow families to approach challenges calmly and find solutions together.

Resolution through play also teaches forgiveness and patience. When families come together to have fun, they develop a sense of humility and learn the importance of letting go of past conflicts. Through laughter and joy, they can move past challenges and strengthen their relationships.

4. Reinforce

Playing together reinforces important family values such as love, respect, and teamwork. **Deuteronomy 6:6-7** says, *"These commandments that I give you today are to be on your hearts. Impress them on your children. Talk about them when you sit at home and when you walk along the road, when you lie down and when you get up."* Games offer parents an opportunity to teach these values in a fun and memorable way.

Family games also reinforce bonds by creating shared experiences. As members work together, they learn to appreciate one another's strengths and talents. **Ecclesiastes 4:9-10** reminds us, *"Two are better than one, because they have a good return for their labor: If either of them falls down, one can help the other up."* Teamwork and encouragement during games help strengthen family unity.

Furthermore, engaging in fun activities reinforces the importance of spending quality time together. They remind families to prioritize their relationships and invest in each other. Games strengthen the foundation of the home, ensuring that love and respect remain at the center of family life.

5. Reconnection

Family games help reconnect members who may feel distant due to busy schedules or misunderstandings. **Malachi 4:6** says, *"He will turn the hearts of the parents to their children, and the hearts of the children to their parents."* Playing together creates moments of connection and understanding, bringing the family closer.

Reconnection through games enables family members to rebuild trust and foster better communication. When everyone participates and shares joy, barriers are broken, and relationships are restored.

1 Thessalonians 5:11 encourages us, *"Therefore encourage one another and build each other up, just as in fact you are doing."* Playtime helps families rediscover their love and appreciation for one another.

Lastly, games remind families that time spent together is precious. They provide an opportunity to set aside differences and focus on what matters most—love, unity, and togetherness. Reconnection through play fosters a sense of belonging, making the home a place of warmth and joy.

6. Relaxation

Playing games brings relaxation to the family, helping members unwind and enjoy each other's company. **Psalm 23:2** says, *"He makes me lie down in green pastures; He leads me beside quiet waters."* Relaxing together strengthens relationships and creates a peaceful atmosphere at home.

Relaxation through games helps reduce stress and improve emotional well-being. Laughter and fun provide a break from the pressures of daily life. **Matthew 11:28** reminds us, *"Come to me, all you who are weary and burdened, and I will give you rest."* Families that take time to relax and play together find refreshment and joy.

Relaxing together also allows families to deepen their connections and share meaningful moments. It reminds everyone to cherish their time with loved ones and find peace in the simplicity of being together. Relaxation through play strengthens the home and creates lasting memories.

7. Ritual

Games can become family rituals that strengthen bonds and create traditions. **Joshua 24:15** says, *"But as for me and my household, we will serve the Lord."* Establishing a tradition of playing games together reinforces the family's commitment to love and unity.

Rituals bring a sense of stability and consistency to the home. They remind families of their shared values and create opportunities for regular connection. **Psalm 145:4** says, *"One generation commends Your works to another; they tell of Your mighty acts."* Family rituals pass down joy and memories from one generation to the next.

Finally, rituals foster a sense of identity and belonging within the family. They help members feel connected and remind them of their unique role in the family. Rituals created through games and play bring joy and meaning to family life.

8. Relief

Playing games provides relief from the stresses and challenges of daily life. **Proverbs 17:22** says, *"A cheerful heart is good medicine, but a crushed spirit dries up the bones."* Games help families relax, laugh, and focus on the joy of being together, providing a much-needed break.

Relief through play also helps families handle difficult emotions. Games bring moments of lightheartedness that encourage healing and comfort. **2 Corinthians 1:4** reminds us that God *"comforts us in all our troubles, so that we can comfort those in any trouble with the comfort we ourselves receive from God."* Fun activities create opportunities to support one another and find relief together.

Lastly, games provide relief by reminding families to focus on the positive. They help shift the perspective from worries to gratitude, strengthening emotional resilience. Relief through play fosters hope and happiness in the home.

9. Recovery

Family games promote recovery by restoring relationships and renewing energy. **Psalm 51:12** says, *"Restore to me the joy of Your salvation and grant me a willing spirit, to sustain me."* Playtime allows families to recover from misunderstandings and rebuild bonds of love and trust.

Recovery through play also strengthens the family's emotional health. Games provide a safe space for members to express their feelings and find encouragement. **Isaiah 40:31** reminds us, *"But those who hope in the Lord will renew their strength."* Families that play together experience healing and renewal.

Additionally, games help families recover from the fatigue of daily life. They bring joy and laughter, reminding everyone of the blessings they share. Recovery through play creates a foundation of peace and love that strengthens the home.

10. Rediscovery

Playing games allows families to rediscover each other's strengths, talents, and uniqueness. **Romans 12:6** reminds us, *"We have different gifts, according to the grace given to each of us."* Games provide an opportunity for family members to celebrate one another's abilities and appreciate what makes each person special.

Rediscovery through play also strengthens relationships by encouraging deeper connections. Families learn more about each other's interests and personalities, fostering understanding and love. **Proverbs 20:5** says, *"The purposes of a person ' s heart are deep waters, but one who has insight draws them out."* Games help families explore and appreciate the depths of each other's hearts.

Lastly, rediscovery brings fresh energy and excitement to the home. It reminds families of the joy of being together and helps them see the blessings they share. Rediscovery through play creates a home filled with love, gratitude, and unity, drawing everyone closer to one another and to God.

12. SIT AND SEARCH YOURSELF

Self-evaluation is a powerful tool for every family, as no family is perfect. It is important to take time to assess how the family functions and how each member contributes to its happiness and growth. **Psalm 139:23-24** says, *"Search me, God, and know my heart; test me and know my anxious thoughts. See if there is any offensive way in me, and lead me in the way everlasting."* This verse reminds us to reflect on ourselves honestly and allow God to guide us toward positive change. Self-evaluation helps families recognize areas where they can improve and grow together. It is a key to progress, reminding us that as family members, we are always learning and evolving.

In a family, no one is an expert, and everyone makes mistakes. **Proverbs 24:16** says, *"For though the righteous fall seven times, they rise again."* We should not be too harsh on ourselves or on one another. Families should learn from their mistakes and even from the errors of others. Being part of a family is a blessing, and it is natural to stumble. What matters most is choosing to learn from these moments and move forward. One of the most important practices in keeping a family happy is forgiveness. **Ephesians 4:32** encourages us, *"Be kind and compassionate to one another, forgiving each other, just as in Christ God forgave you."* Forgiveness helps family members live in peace, heal from hurt, and strengthen their relationships.

Each member of the family needs to sit and reflect on their own contributions. Ask questions like, "How am I doing? Am I really helping to make the family better?" Self-reflection fosters accountability and encourages individuals to play an active role in their family's well-being. **James 1:19** says, *"Everyone should be quick to listen, slow to speak, and slow to become angry."* When families gather to talk and share their thoughts, many issues can be solved peacefully. These conversations strengthen family unity and bring a deeper understanding of one another. Self-evaluation is vital for achieving success, stability, and strength within the family.

Before we complain or point fingers, we need to count our blessings and correct our own mistakes. Jesus reminds us in **Matthew 7:3**, *"Why do you look at the speck of sawdust in your* brother ' s eye and pay no attention to the plank in your own eye?" Instead of focusing on others' shortcomings, we should examine our own actions and ensure we are doing what is right. When one family member messes up, it is the responsibility of the others to offer support, help them heal, and restore harmony to the home. **Galatians 6:2** says, "Carry each other's burdens, and in this way, you will fulfill the law of Christ." By helping and encouraging one another, families grow stronger and remain united, building a home filled with love and understanding

Self-evaluation is a valuable way for families to strengthen their relationships and improve. When family members take the time to reflect on their actions, it helps them understand themselves better. **Proverbs 4:7** says, *"The beginning of wisdom is this: Get wisdom. Though it cost all you have, get understanding."* By reflecting on their own behavior, they can identify areas for improvement and become better. This helps family members grow and take responsibility for their actions. It also makes relationships stronger because each person tries their best to support the family and avoid mistakes.

Another benefit of self-evaluation is that it helps solve problems and brings peace to the home. Families who reflect on their behavior can learn how to resolve conflicts more easily. **Ephesians 4:2** says, *"Be completely humble and gentle; be patient, bearing with one another in love."* When family members reflect on how they have treated each other, it fosters empathy and understanding. Self-evaluation helps create a loving and supportive environment where everyone feels valued. Families can sit together, talk openly, and find ways to grow closer.

Finally, self-evaluation reminds families to count their blessings. Before pointing fingers or complaining, it's important to reflect on your own actions and thank God for His blessings. **Matthew 7:3** reminds us, "*Why do you look at the speck of sawdust in your brother' s eye and pay no attention to the plank in your own eye?*" Families should focus on correcting their own mistakes and supporting one another through challenges. When one person struggles, the family can come together to help and heal. Self-evaluation fosters unity, strength, and peace, creating a happy and loving home environment.

14

THE BENEFITS OF SELF-EVALUATION

1. Rate Yourself

S elf-evaluation begins with rating yourself honestly in your role within the family. This means taking a moment to assess how you have been contributing to the home. Are you being helpful, supportive, and kind? **Galatians 6:4** says, *"Each one should test their own actions. Then they can take pride in themselves alone, without comparing themselves to someone else."* By rating yourself, you gain a better understanding of your strengths and areas where you need improvement. This helps you grow as a family member and encourages you to focus on making positive changes.

Rating yourself also builds self-awareness. When you evaluate your actions, you see the impact you have on your family members. It reminds you of the importance of being thoughtful and intentional in your words and deeds. Instead of blaming others for family struggles, you become more accountable for your part in maintaining peace and happiness. This practice fosters growth and cultivates a more loving and understanding home environment.

2. Reflect on Your Progress and Behavior

Reflection is an important part of self-evaluation. It enables you to reflect deeply on your progress and behavior as a family member. **Lamentations 3:40** says, *"Let us examine our ways and test them, and let us return to the Lord."* This verse shows that reflecting on your actions is not only helpful but also a spiritual practice. By looking back on how you've treated others, handled conflicts, and supported the family, you can identify areas where you've grown and areas where you can do better.

Reflection also brings clarity to your relationships. It helps you understand the feelings of your family members and how your behavior affects them. This process fosters empathy and strengthens connections, allowing you to make thoughtful adjustments that improve family unity. By taking time to reflect, you become more patient and considerate, which in turn contributes to a happier and more peaceful home.

3. Redefine and Re-examine Your Actions

Self-evaluation encourages you to redefine your role and re-examine your actions as part of the family. This means asking yourself questions like, "Am I doing enough to support my family?" and "How can I improve as a parent, sibling, or child?" **Romans 12:2** reminds us, *'Do not conform to the pattern of this world, but be transformed by the renewing of your mind."* Redefining your role helps you focus on positive habits and values that benefit the entire family.

Re-examining your actions also helps you recognize mistakes and correct them. When you take an honest look at how you've been acting, you can identify areas where you've fallen short and work on making changes. This builds accountability and helps you contribute to a more united and loving family. By redefining and re-examining your role, you set a strong foundation for better relationships and growth within the home.

4. Realize the Impact of Your Actions

Through self-evaluation, you can recognize how significantly your actions impact your family. Every word, decision, and behavior contributes to the harmony and happiness of the home. **Ephesians 4:2-3** says, *"Be completely humble and gentle; be patient, bearing with one another in love. Make every effort to keep the unity of the Spirit through the bond of peace."* When you realize the importance of your role, you understand that you have the power to bring peace, love, and understanding to your family. Recognizing your impact encourages you to act with care and intention.

Realizing your role helps you appreciate how much each family member matters. It reminds you to focus on your strengths while working on areas that need improvement. Instead of being overly critical of yourself or others, self-evaluation encourages growth. As **Galatians 6:4** reminds us, *"Each one should test their own actions. Then they can take pride in themselves alone, without comparing themselves to someone else."* By understanding the effect of your actions, you become more thoughtful and contribute positively to the family.

When you realize your value in the family, it motivates you to treat others with love and respect. Acknowledging your responsibilities and efforts builds stronger connections and unity.

This process fosters gratitude for the gift of family and inspires you to work toward a more harmonious home. Recognizing the significance of your role helps you take proactive steps to make your family a happier and stronger unit.

5. Renew Your Commitment to Your Family

Self-evaluation also allows you to renew your commitment to your family. This means deciding to love, support, and help your family even more. Renewing your commitment involves making an intentional effort to strengthen your relationships and create a peaceful home. **Colossians 3:13** encourages, *"Bear with each other and forgive one another if any of you has a grievance against someone. Forgive as the Lord forgave you."* When you renew your dedication, you focus on building unity and forgiving past mistakes.

Renewing your commitment also means setting new goals for how you can contribute to your family. For example, you might decide to spend more time together, communicate more effectively, or assist more with daily responsibilities. A renewed commitment inspires others in your family to follow your example. Your efforts create an effect of love, patience, and cooperation. **Proverbs 16:3** says, *"Commit to the Lord whatever you do, and He will establish your plans."* With God's guidance, your dedication can bring amazing changes to your home.

Consistency is key when renewing your commitment. Families grow stronger when each member makes an ongoing effort to contribute positively. By renewing your commitment regularly, you can ensure your family remains united and full of love. This not only strengthens family relationships but also helps create a happy and peaceful home where everyone feels valued and cared for.

Renewing your commitment brings fresh energy and purpose to your role in the family.

6. Resolve to Improve

Finally, self-evaluation encourages you to resolve to improve and take steps toward becoming a better family member. **James 1:22** says, *"Do not merely listen to the word, and so deceive yourselves. Do what it says."* Resolving to improve means putting into action what you' ve learned during self-reflection. Whether it's being more patient, helping with chores more often, or communicating more openly, every small change makes a significant difference.

Resolving to improve also teaches forgiveness and understanding within the family. When one member takes steps to grow, it inspires others to do the same. This fosters a supportive and loving environment where everyone collaborates to overcome challenges. With God's guidance and your commitment to growth, resolving to improve helps create a home filled with peace, joy, and love.

15

BE GOOD AT COMMUNICATION

Communication is very important for a happy and healthy family. The way we speak to our family members matters a great deal because our words and actions reveal how much we value and appreciate them. Sadly, some family members take each other for granted, forgetting that having family is a blessing from God. **Psalm 133:1** reminds us, *"How good and pleasant it is when God ' s people live together in unity!"* Each family member is a gift, and our perception of our family should be positive. Treasure your family, knowing there are no perfect families, but God put you together for a reason. Always try your best to be kind and supportive. Communicating well lets your family feel loved and appreciated, building a stronger and happier home.

Good communication is the key to creating understanding in the family. It helps reduce conflicts and builds trust, unity, and calmness. **Proverbs 15:1** teaches, *"A gentle answer turns away wrath, but a harsh word stirs up anger."* When we communicate kindly, we show love and respect to one another. Good communication also makes it easier to solve problems and navigate challenges as a family.

When family members share their thoughts and feelings openly, they create an environment where everyone feels safe and valued. It helps to strengthen relationships, bringing peace and joy to the home.

To improve communication at home, start by practicing active listening. **James 1:19** says, *"Everyone should be quick to listen, slow to speak and slow to become angry."* Listening carefully to each other shows that you care about their thoughts and feelings. Value and treat each family member with kindness, knowing that everyone deserves love and respect. Simple acts, like making eye contact, nodding, and giving your full attention, make a big difference. Showing that you are listening builds trust and helps prevent misunderstandings.

Remember that God calls us to love one another deeply within the family. **John 13:34** reminds us, *"A new command I give you: Love one another. As I have loved you, so you must love one another."* You are the best person to show love to your family members through your words and actions. Let your communication be full of grace, patience, and kindness. By improving the way you talk and listen to each other, you can create a home filled with unity, trust, and happiness. Let God guide your conversations, and your family will grow stronger together.

MAKE GREAT COMMUNICATION

1. Respect

Respect is the foundation of good communication in a family. **Ephesians 4:29** says, *"Do not let any unwholesome talk come out of your mouths, but only what is helpful for building others up according to their needs."* Respect means speaking to family members with kindness and valuing their feelings and opinions. It

SYAVIHA MULENGYA

shows that you care about them and are willing to listen. When respect is present, communication becomes more positive, and everyone feels valued and appreciated.

Respect also means avoiding hurtful words or actions. **Proverbs 15:1** reminds us, *"A gentle answer turns away wrath, but a harsh word stirs up anger."* Harsh words can damage relationships, while respectful communication creates peace and understanding. By choosing to be respectful, you show your love for your family and help create a harmonious home.

Finally, respect encourages mutual trust. When family members respect one another, they feel safe expressing their thoughts and emotions. This builds stronger connections and helps solve conflicts peacefully. Respect in communication strengthens the family and fosters a loving environment where everyone feels valued.

2. Responsible

Being responsible in communication means taking ownership of your words and actions. **Proverbs 18:21** says, *"The tongue has the power of life and death, and those who love it will eat its fruit."* Words have a great impact, and being responsible means using them wisely to build relationships rather than harm them. Take a moment to think before you speak and ensure your words convey kindness and encouragement.

Responsibility also involves being honest and truthful in your communication. **Ephesians 4:25** says, *"Therefore each of you must put off falsehood and speak truthfully to your neighbor, for we are all members of one body."* Honesty builds trust and strengthens relationships within the family. Avoid blame and instead focus on finding solutions to problems. Taking responsibility for your mistakes and apologizing when necessary demonstrates maturity and a genuine care for others.

Lastly, responsible communication means being reliable and consistent. Show your family that you mean what you say by keeping your promises and following through on your commitments. This builds trust and creates a dependable and supportive family environment where communication thrives.

3. Reciprocity

Reciprocity in communication means giving and receiving equally. **Luke 6:31** says, *"Do to others as you would have them do to you."* Treat family members the way you want to be treated, listening to them with the same care and attention you expect in return. Communication should be a two-way street where everyone feels heard and understood.

Reciprocity fosters fairness and balance in relationships. When family members communicate openly and respectfully, it strengthens their bond. **Galatians 6:2** reminds us, *"Carry each other's burdens, and in this way, you will fulfill the law of Christ."* When one person listens and supports another, it creates an atmosphere of love and cooperation.

Additionally, reciprocity encourages understanding and patience. By being willing to listen and respond kindly, family members learn to value each other's feelings. This mutual respect fosters peace and unity within the home, cultivating a loving and supportive family environment.

4. Reasonable

Being reasonable in communication means speaking and listening with fairness and an open mind. **James 1:19** says,

"Everyone should be quick to listen, slow to speak and slow to become angry." This means giving others a chance to explain their thoughts without interrupting or judging. It helps create a calm and respectful conversation where everyone feels valued.

Reasonable communication also means avoiding exaggeration and staying focused on the issue at hand. **Proverbs 12:18** says, *"The words of the reckless pierce like swords, but the tongue of the wise brings healing."* Choosing your words wisely and staying calm helps prevent arguments and resolve conflicts in a healthy way.

Lastly, being reasonable helps in finding solutions that work for everyone. Families should approach problems with understanding and a willingness to compromise. By listening and responding fairly, families can strengthen their relationships and build a peaceful home.

5. Rich in Love

Communication in the family should always be rich in love. **1 Corinthians 13:4-5** reminds us, *"Love is patient, love is kind. It does not envy, it does not boast, it is not proud. It does not dishonor others, it is not self-seeking, it is not easily angered, it keeps no record of wrongs."* Speaking with love means being patient, kind, and gentle in your words, even when discussing difficult issues.

When communication is full of love, it creates a safe and supportive environment. **Ephesians 4:15** says, *"Instead, speaking the truth in love, we will grow to become in every respect the mature body of Him who is the head, that is, Christ."* Speaking the truth with love helps family members build trust and understanding while maintaining respect for one another.

Rich, loving communication also strengthens emotional connections within the family. By expressing care, gratitude, and affection through your words, you deepen your bond with your loved ones. Love-filled communication brings joy, peace, and unity to the home, reflecting God's love for all of us.

6. Resourceful

Resourceful communication involves finding creative and effective ways to solve problems and build connections within the family. **Proverbs 3:5-6** encourages us, *"Trust in the Lord with all your heart and lean not on your own understanding; in all your ways submit to Him, and He will make your paths straight."* By seeking God's wisdom, families can develop solutions to challenges and improve their communication.

Being resourceful means utilizing tools such as family meetings, clear schedules, and shared activities to enhance communication. These strategies allow family members to spend time together and share their thoughts openly. Resourcefulness also means finding ways to make conversations engaging and productive, such as playing games or engaging in storytelling to strengthen bonds.

Resourceful communication is about being adaptable and willing to try new approaches. **Ecclesiastes 4:9** says, *"Two are better than one, because they have a good return for their labor."* When families work together creatively, they discover new ways to connect, solve problems, and grow stronger. Resourceful communication ensures that the family continues to thrive and face challenges with unity and love.

16

SIMPLE STEPS, STRONGER BONDS: WHAT TRULY MATTERS AT HOME

The small things in a family matter greatly because they contribute to a loving and happy home. It is important to remember that you are the builder of your family, and there is no stranger who will come to build it for you. **Proverbs 24:3** reminds us, *"By wisdom a house is built, and through understanding it is established."* Building a great family doesn't require big things; instead, it's the small actions that bring joy and lasting impact. Simple gestures, such as saying thank you or showing appreciation, make family members feel valued and loved. A happy home starts with these little things.

Taking time to share meals is another small yet powerful way to strengthen family bonds. Sitting together, talking, and laughing over food creates meaningful moments that everyone cherishes. **Acts 2:46** says, *"They broke bread in their homes and ate together with glad and sincere hearts."* Sharing meals fosters unity and creates opportunities for deeper connection. A hug, a smile, or a kind word can bring immense joy and convey love. These little actions remind family members that they are cared for and appreciated.

Listening attentively to one another is key to creating a peaceful and happy family. **James 1:19** encourages, "Be quick to listen, slow to speak and slow to become angry." Taking time to truly hear your family members shows respect and builds trust. Complimenting each other is another small act that makes a big difference. Words like "You are amazing," or "I'm proud of you," bring confidence and positivity to the home. Cherishing one another creates an environment of love and kindness that strengthens the family.

Finding small ways to show thoughtfulness can make your family happier. Leave little notes with messages like "I love you" or "You're the best," to brighten someone's day. Laughing together is also a wonderful way to bond and bring joy into the home. **Proverbs 17:22** says, *"A cheerful heart is good medicine."* Helping out without being asked shows kindness and builds teamwork within the family. Small surprises or honoring special days create moments of happiness that bring the family closer.

Celebrating small wins is another way to make the home joyful. Recognizing each other's achievements, no matter how small, shows support and encouragement. **Romans 12:15** reminds us, *"Rejoice with those who rejoice."* Celebrating creates positive memories and strengthens the bond between family members. Saying "I miss you," or "You mean so much to me," reminds family members how important they are. These small words bring comfort and build trust.

Start small, start somewhere. The small things you do can make a big difference in your family. **Proverbs 18:21** says, *"The tongue has the power of life and death."* Use your words and actions to build a great and happy family, one small step at a time. By choosing to show love, kindness, and appreciation, you create the family you want—a home filled with love, unity, and joy. Let God guide your efforts, and you'll see the blessings in your family grow.

The Power of Small: Making Home a Place of Peace and Purpose

1. Greetings

A warm greeting may seem like a small gesture, but its impact on family life is incredibly meaningful. Taking the time to say "good morning," "hello," or "how was your day?" shows your care and attention to the people you love. **Proverbs 15:23** reminds us, *"A person finds joy in giving an apt reply—and how good is a timely word!"* Simple words of acknowledgment create positivity and let your family know that you value their presence. Even during busy or stressful times, a friendly greeting can brighten someone's mood and strengthen the bond between family members.

Greeting one another also reflects respect and thoughtfulness. It reminds everyone in the family that they are appreciated and loved. A warm greeting, coupled with a smile, adds an extra layer of kindness that fosters trust and connection. **Colossians 4:6** advises us, *"Let your conversation be always full of grace, seasoned with salt, so that you may know how to answer everyone."* Showing respect and grace through greetings creates a welcoming environment where family members feel comfortable and safe. When a family actively embraces this habit, the home becomes a place of peace and comfort.

Greetings are also the starting point of healthy communication within a family. They open the door to meaningful conversations and provide an opportunity to check in with one another. Asking "how are you?" and genuinely listening to the answer lets your family know they are valued and cared for. **Proverbs 18:13** warns, *"To answer before listening—that is folly and shame."* By using greetings as a means of connection, families can share moments of joy and support one another in times of need. These interactions build deeper relationships and strengthen the unity of the home.

Finally, consistent and heartfelt greetings contribute to a loving and joyful atmosphere. Making it a daily habit to greet your family warmly develops an environment of affection and closeness. It's a simple way to show that you prioritize your relationships and are invested in building a strong and harmonious family life. Greetings may seem small, but they carry the power to transform a home into a sanctuary of love and positivity where everyone feels cherished. By putting effort into this small act, you can create lasting connections and cultivate a truly happy home.

2. Generosity

Generosity is a powerful way to build love and unity in a family. **Acts 20:35** reminds us, *"It is more blessed to give than to receive."* Generosity can be expressed in many ways, such as sharing time, helping with chores, or offering kind words. It shows your family members that you care about their needs and are willing to prioritize their happiness. Even small acts of generosity, such as sharing a snack or lending a helping hand, can foster a sense of togetherness and support.

Being generous also means offering your forgiveness and understanding. Families are not perfect, and mistakes will happen. **Proverbs 11:25** says, *"A generous person will prosper; whoever refreshes others will be refreshed."* By being patient and forgiving, you create an environment of love and peace where everyone feels accepted. Generosity in attitude and actions strengthens the family bond and helps resolve conflicts.

Lastly, generosity teaches valuable life lessons to children and other family members. It encourages them to think about others and develop kindness and empathy. A generous family builds a legacy of love and compassion that extends beyond the home. By practicing generosity, you bless your family and create a home filled with joy and harmony.

3. Guidance

Guidance is essential for creating a strong and happy family. **Proverbs 22:6** says, *"Start children off on the way they should go, and even when they are old, they will not turn from it."* Guiding your family means offering advice, support, and wisdom to help them make good decisions. Parents can guide their children by teaching them values and principles, while siblings can support each other through life's challenges. Guidance helps family members grow into confident and responsible individuals.

Guidance also involves listening and understanding. When you take the time to hear your family's concerns, you show them that you care about their well-being. **Psalm 119:105** says, *"Your word is a lamp for my feet, a light on my path."* Sharing God's teachings and wisdom with your family provides a foundation for growth and strength. Guidance brings clarity and peace, helping family members navigate difficult situations with confidence.

Lastly, guidance creates a sense of purpose and direction within the family. It helps everyone understand their role and responsibilities while encouraging teamwork and cooperation. By providing loving guidance, you build a supportive and united home that reflects God's love and grace.

4. Gifts

Giving gifts is a simple yet effective way to show love and appreciation within a family. **James 1:17** says, *"Every good and perfect gift is from above, coming down from the Father of the heavenly lights."* Gifts don't need to be extravagant to be meaningful—a thoughtful note, a favorite treat, or a small surprise can bring joy to your loved ones. Giving a gift shows that you've thought about someone and want to make them happy.

Gifts also strengthen family relationships by celebrating special moments. Birthdays, milestones, or even an ordinary day can become an occasion to express your love. **Romans 12:6** reminds us, *"We have different gifts, according to the grace given to each of us."* Sharing gifts helps family members feel valued and appreciated, creating a positive atmosphere of care and gratitude.

Lastly, gifts reflect God's generosity toward us and remind us to share His blessings with others. **Acts 20:35** teaches, *"It is more blessed to give than to receive."* Through giving, families can build a home filled with kindness, joy, and love that grows stronger with every thoughtful gesture.

5. Game

Playing games together is a joyful way to bring the family closer. **Ecclesiastes 3:4** says, *"A time to weep and a time to laugh, a time to mourn and a time to dance."* Games encourage laughter and fun, creating happy memories and strengthening family bonds. Whether it's a board game, card game, or outdoor activity, playing together fosters teamwork and communication.

Games also teach important lessons such as patience, problem-solving, and cooperation. **Proverbs 17:22** reminds us, *"A cheerful heart is good medicine."* Games offer a chance for families to relax and enjoy each other's company, bringing positivity and energy into the home. These small moments of connection build trust and unity.

Additionally, family game time offers an opportunity to break away from daily routines and spend quality time together. It reminds everyone to appreciate the gift of family and the joy of shared experiences. By making time for games, families can create a loving and supportive environment where happiness flourishes.

6. Gathering

Gathering as a family is vital for creating unity and connection. **Hebrews 10:25** encourages us, *"Not giving up meeting together, as some are in the habit of doing, but encouraging one another."* Whether it's for a meal, a celebration, or a casual conversation, spending time together strengthens bonds and fosters a sense of belonging.

Family gatherings offer opportunities to share experiences, laugh together, and offer mutual support. Sitting down to eat or talk allows everyone to feel included and valued. **Ecclesiastes 4:9** reminds us, *"Two are better than one, because they have a good return for their labor."* Gathering brings families closer and fosters love and understanding.

Moreover, gatherings help families create lasting memories and celebrate their blessings. They remind everyone of the importance of being present and connected. Regular family gatherings build a strong foundation for love, unity, and happiness at home.

7. Gratitude

Gratitude is a small but powerful way to bring joy and peace into a family. Taking time to say "thank you" to your loved ones shows that you appreciate their efforts and value their presence in your life. **1 Thessalonians 5:18** reminds us, *"Give thanks in all circumstances; for this is God's will for you in Christ Jesus."* When you thank your family members for the little things they do, it encourages kindness and cooperation. This simple gesture reminds everyone that their contributions, no matter how small, are noticed and appreciated, which strengthens the bond within the family.

Practicing gratitude creates a positive and uplifting atmosphere in the home. It helps family members focus on their blessings rather than dwelling on challenges or frustrations. Being thankful teaches contentment and helps everyone find joy in what they have rather than longing for what they don't. Gratitude also helps shift the focus toward God's provision and care for the family. By remembering to express gratitude, families build a stronger connection to one another and to God, fostering a sense of peace and harmony within the home.

Finally, gratitude deepens faith and unity within the family. When families take the time to thank God for His blessings, they grow closer to Him and to each other. Gratitude brings hearts together and reminds the family of God's grace and love in their lives. **Ephesians 5:20** encourages us to be *"always giving thanks to God the Father for everything."* By creating a habit of gratitude, families build a strong foundation of love and happiness that transforms their home into a place of joy and togetherness.

8. Going Out

Going out together as a family is a small act that can have a big impact on creating a happy and united home. Spending time outside the house—whether it's a simple walk in the park, a fun outing, or a visit to a favorite restaurant—helps strengthen family bonds. **Ecclesiastes 3:1** reminds us, "There is a time for everything, and a season for every activity under the heavens." Going out together allows families to share joyful moments and create lasting memories, reminding each member of the importance of their connection.

When families go out together, they escape the distractions of daily routines and focus on each other. This quality time builds communication and understanding as they enjoy activities side by side. **Proverbs 27:17** says, *"As iron sharpens iron, so one person sharpens another."* Spending time outdoors fosters teamwork, whether it involves hiking, playing games, or exploring new places. These moments strengthen trust and create opportunities for laughter and shared experiences.

Going out as a family also helps relieve stress and renew energy. A change of scenery brings fresh perspectives and positivity, improving the emotional well-being of every member. Spending time in nature or engaging in fun activities helps restore peace and joy within the family. **Psalm 19:1** reminds us, *"The heavens declare the glory of God; the skies proclaim the work of His hands."* Appreciating God's creation together strengthens both faith and relationships. By prioritizing outings and activities, families can celebrate the small joys of life while building a stronger, happier home.

9. Grace

Showing grace is essential for maintaining peace and harmony in the family. **Colossians 3:13** says, *"Bear with each other and forgive one another if any of you has a grievance against someone. Forgive as the Lord forgave you."* Grace involves being patient, kind, and forgiving toward family members, even when mistakes are made.

Grace helps resolve conflicts and strengthens relationships. Instead of holding on to anger, choosing grace brings healing and unity. It teaches family members to support each other with love and compassion, creating an environment of understanding.

Grace also reflects God's love in the home. **Ephesians 4:32** reminds us, *"Be kind and compassionate to one another, forgiving each other, just as in Christ God forgave you."* By practicing grace, families create a caring and peaceful atmosphere where everyone feels accepted and loved.

Prayer for a Friendly and Happy Home

Dear Heavenly Father, Thank You for the gift of family and the blessing of a home. I pray that You fill our house with love, laughter, and peace. Help us to treat one another with kindness, respect, and patience. May our words build up and not tear down. Teach us to listen, forgive, and support each other daily. Let our home be a place where Your presence is felt and Your joy is shared. Lord, guide us to be a friendly family—welcoming, warm, and united. May our relationships grow stronger through Your wisdom and grace. Let our home reflect Your love and be a light to others. In Jesus' name, we pray. Amen.

Prayer of Confession and Invitation to God

Dear Lord, I confess that I have not always put You first in my heart or in my home. Forgive me for the times I allowed anger, pride, or fear to take Your place. Today, I open my heart to You. Come in, Lord Jesus, and be the center of my life and my family. Cleanse us, renew us, and lead us in Your truth. I invite You into every room of our home—fill it with Your peace, Your power, and Your presence. Teach us to walk in love, live in faith, and grow in grace. May our home be a dwelling place for Your Spirit and a reflection of heaven on earth. In Jesus' name, Amen.

BY SYAVIHA MULENGYA

Before The last Page ,

Other Books By Syaviha Mulengya

1. All Who Comes Are Welcome
2. Better Than Them
3. Best Secret for Greatness
4. Break Free, Live Free
5. Did You Get the Gift?
6. His Battle, Your Victory
7. I Want the Best for My Child
8. It Is You, Not Me
9. Just Ask Like Jabez
10. Knowing the King of Kings Is Key
11. Love Your Life, Live Your Life
12. Men Are Crying, Women Are Weeping
13. No Matter What, You Matter So Much
14. Rate Yourself
15. Secrets for Singles
16. Secrets for Success for Teens and Youth
17. Stronger Than Your Struggles
18. Treasure Your Blessings
19. Work, Wait, and Win
20. What Makes the World So Sweet
21. Yes to His Voice, No to the Noise
22. You Are a Winner, Why Worry?
23. You Have a Bright Future, Do Not Give Up
24. Your Best Secret

www.ingramcontent.com/pod-product-compliance
Lightning Source LLC
Chambersburg PA
CBHW061807120626
46550CB00005B/2182